Toolkit Texts

Selected by **Stephanie Harvey** and **Anne Goudvis**

Short Nonfiction for American History
Colonial Times

1600　　1625　　1650　　1675　　1700　　1725　　1750

*first*hand

HEINEMANN

DEDICATED TO TEACHERS™

DEDICATED TO TEACHERS™

Heinemann
361 Hanover Street
Portsmouth, NH 03801-3912
www.heinemann.com

Offices and agents throughout the world

Cataloging-in-Publishing Data for this book is available from the Library of Congress

Editor: Heather Anderson
Production: Stephanie J. Levy
Cover Design: Suzanne Heiser
Typesetter: Eclipse Publishing Services
Manufacturing: Steve Bernier

ISBN 10: 0-325-04883-5
ISBN 13: 978-0-325-04883-3

Printed in the United States of America on acid-free paper
18 17 16 15 14 EBM 1 2 3 4 5

Acknowledgments

The *Comprehension Toolkit* series is all about collaboration. None of this would be possible without the commitment, diligence, and hard work of our Heinemann team. We are very grateful to Heather Anderson, Stephanie Levy, Tina Miller, Anita Gildea, Charles McQuillen, David Stirling, and Steven Bernier for the energy, creative thinking, and hard work that has brought this resource to life. We thank the entire Heinemann team for their enthusiasm and ongoing support of our work.

— Steph and Anne

Contents

Lessons for Close Reading in History

Articles

If you lived in Colonial America, then you were alive during an exciting time. Of course, how you felt about these times depended on who you were, where you were living, and what you did. Native Americans, colonists from many countries, enslaved people, and indentured servants all experienced this time of change differently.

FIRST ENCOUNTERS IN THE NEW WORLD

Explorers set sail from England for the New World with dreams of gold, silver, and new lands to colonize. But it wasn't as easy as simply sailing across the ocean.

Sailing on a ship was not an easy way to travel. There were hurricanes, diseases, not enough food, and often pirates, too.

NEW ENGLAND COLONIES

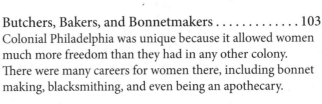

MIDDLE COLONIES

Colonial Philadelphia was unique because it allowed women
much more freedom than they had in any other colony.
There were many careers for women there, including bonnet
making, blacksmithing, and even being an apothecary.

Maryland, with its tobacco and corn crops, needed a great
deal of labor. At first indentured servants came to earn their
freedom, but eventually indentured servitude would be
replaced by the institution of slavery.

Molly Bannaky was an indentured servant who earned her freedom and married
an enslaved African. Her grandson, Benjamin Banneker, would become a famous
astronomer and surveyor, helping to survey the city of Washington, D.C.

Taking a walk through Philadelphia three hundred years ago would
be a shock. Farm animals roamed the muddy streets, and pickpockets
were quick to steal from pedestrians who didn't pay attention.

The first Africans came to New Amsterdam as slaves only a few years
after the city was founded by the Dutch in 1624. Some would earn
their freedom and become landowners.

SOUTHERN COLONIES

Nyack, a fictional child whose name means "I won't give up," came to America on a
slave ship in 1619 after being captured in Africa and forced into slavery along with
his family.

Thomas and Susannah Bridges, fictional characters, describe their life as indentured
servants in Jamestown. Life was not easy for orphans at this time.

During Jamestown's first 17 years, hundreds of children were sent there, often without
their parents. Some even became interpreters and ambassadors between settlers and
the Powhatan tribe.

INVESTIGATING HISTORY THROUGH ARCHAEOLOGY

The **DIGITAL COMPANION RESOURCE** includes:

- all of the articles in full color,
- primary source documents,
- a full-color image bank, and
- "Teaching for Historical Literacy," by Anne Goudvis and Stephanie Harvey (Educational Leadership, March 2012).

For instructions on how to access the Digital Companion Resource, turn to
page xviii.

Introduction

Reading, writing, viewing, listening, talking, and investigating are the hallmarks of active literacy. Throughout the school day and across the curriculum, kids are actively inferring, questioning, discussing, debating, inquiring, and generating new ideas. An active literacy classroom fairly bursts with enthusiastic, engaged learning.

The same goes for our history and social studies classrooms: They, too, must be thinking- and learning-intensive (Harvard College, 2007). To build intrigue, knowledge, and understanding in history, students read and learn about the events, mysteries, questions, controversies, issues, discoveries, and drama that are the real stuff of history.

Disciplinary Literacy

When students acquire knowledge in a discipline such as history and think about what they are learning, new insights and understandings emerge and kids generate new knowledge. Fundamental to this understanding is the idea that there's a difference between information and knowledge. Kids have to construct their own knowledge: only they can turn information into knowledge by thinking about it. But we educators must provide the environment, resources, and instruction so kids become curious, active learners.

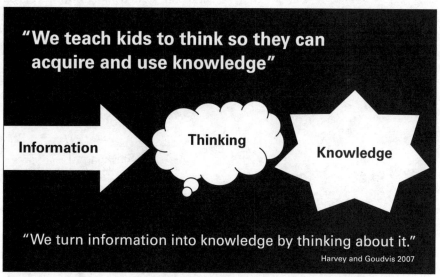

From Anne Goudvis, Stephanie Harvey, Brad Buhrow, and Anne Upczak-Garcia, 2012. *Scaffolding the Comprehension Toolkit for English Language Learners.* Portsmouth, New Hampshire: Heinemann.

But too often students experience history as a passive slog through the textbook, with a "coverage" curriculum that's a mile wide and an inch deep. Instead, students should be reading and actively responding to a wide range of historical sources; viewing and analyzing images; reading historical fiction, first-person accounts, letters, and all manner of sources, so they can understand and empathize with the experiences of people who lived "long ago and far away."

In this approach to disciplinary literacy, students use reading and thinking strategies as tools to acquire knowledge in history, science, and other subject areas. P. David Pearson and colleagues (Pearson, Moje, and Greenleaf, 2010) suggest that:

> Without systematic attention to reading and writing in subjects like science and history, students will leave schools with an impoverished sense of what it means to use the tools of literacy for learning or even to reason within various disciplines. (p. 460)

Reading and thinking about historical sources and introducing students to ways of thinking in the discipline of history teaches them that there are many ways to understand the people, events, issues, and ideas of the past. But we also want students to understand the power and potential of their own thinking and learning so that they learn to think for themselves and connect history to their own lives.

CONTENT MATTERS

Cervetti, Jaynes, and Hiebert (2009) suggest that reading for understanding is the foundation for students acquiring and using knowledge. In this figure (below), Cervetti et al. explain the reciprocal relationship between knowledge and comprehension—how background knowledge supports comprehension and in turn, through comprehension/reading for understanding, we "build new knowledge" (p. 83).

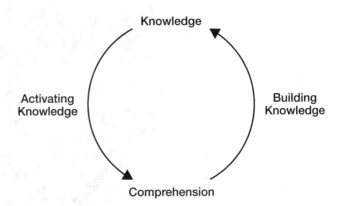

Research (Anderson and Pearson, 1984) has long supported the strong relationship between background knowledge and school learning: Students' prior knowledge about content supports their new learning. From our perspective, history, more than many subjects, demands that students have a context for their learning, that they understand the essential ideas that emerge within a larger time span, and that they can discern the big picture.

But activating background knowledge is just the beginning. Researchers emphasize the knowledge-building side of this figure, which underscores the idea that when we comprehend, we add to and enhance our store of knowledge. "Knowledge, from this perspective, does not refer to a litany of facts, but rather to the discipline-based conceptual understandings … (which) engage students in becoming experts on the world around them." (Cervetti, et al., 2009)

This is a reciprocal process that occurs as students build their knowledge in many content areas and disciplines. P. David Pearson sums it up well with his quip: "Today's new knowledge is tomorrow's background knowledge." The more students know, the more they will learn, and even more important, the more they will want to learn!

Historical Literacy

Our approach is to embed reading and thinking strategies in our social studies and history instruction, so that comprehension and thinking strategies become tools for learning and understanding content. Teaching historical literacy means we merge thoughtful, foundational literacy practices with challenging, engaging resources to immerse kids in historical ways of thinking.

What might this look like?

Students:

- Read and reason through many different kinds of sources about the past, connecting to the experiences, dilemmas, discoveries, and reflections of people from other times and places.

- Ask their own authentic questions, just like historians do.

- Learn to read critically—to understand different purposes and perspectives, asking "Who wrote this? Why did they write it? What are the authors' biases, points of view, and purposes?"

- Try out ways of thinking about history—inferring, analyzing, and interpreting facts and evidence to surface themes and important ideas.

We believe these practices, above all, promote engagement with the discipline and motivate kids to want to find out more. When kids actively read, think, debate, discuss, and investigate, they have the best shot at becoming enthusiastic students of history. Not incidentally, zeroing in on content literacy in this way will go a long way in helping students meet district and state standards, including the Common Core State Standards (CCSS), which focus on 21st century skills and learning across disciplines. The instructional practices advocated in this resource are supported by research that emphasizes a content-rich, standards-based approach:

A multi-source, multi-genre curriculum. We envision the active literacy classroom awash in engaging historical resources of all kinds: maps, timelines, artifacts, songs, poems, journals, letters, feature articles, biographies, and so on. Allington and Johnston (2002) found that students evidenced higher achievement when their classroom focused on a multi-source, multi-genre, multi-perspective curriculum rather than a one-size-fits-all coverage approach.

Standards-based. The CCSS, as well as many state standards, highlight the importance of reading in the disciplines and reading for deeper meaning. Comprehension and thinking strategies are foundational for many of these standards. We don't "teach the standards," of course; we design instruction that supports students to read, reason, and respond so that they meet the appropriate standards. This resource includes ways in which comprehension and thinking strategies further the active use of knowledge and greater understanding in history and social studies.

Social studies strands. This resource provides a range of reading in the different social studies strands: history, culture, economics, government, and geography. A chart correlating the articles to the social studies strands appears on pages xvii and xviii.

History is the study of people, events, and achievements in the past. Learning about history helps students understand how people and societies behave. It also allows students to make connections between themselves and others who lived long ago. In addition, history helps students to understand the process of change and better prepare themselves for changes they will encounter in their lives.

Culture is the customs, traditions, habits, and values of a group of people. Learning about culture helps students to better understand and relate to others. By examining their own cultural traditions, students can understand the values of their society. By examining the cultural institutions of other groups, students can gain an appreciation of people who live differently from themselves and also see similarities they might not have otherwise realized.

Economics is the study of production, distribution, and consumption of goods and services. When students learn about economics, they learn how individuals, groups, and governments all make choices to satisfy their needs and wants. Understanding economics helps students to make better financial decisions in their own lives and also helps them to make sense of the economic world we live in.

Government is a system for making laws and keeping order in a city, state, or country. By learning about government, students are preparing themselves to be good citizens and take part in their political system. Understanding government helps students not only understand the modern-day world and its events; it also gives them the power to change that world through public actions.

Geography is the study of the Earth's surface and features and of the ways in which those features affect people around the world. Understanding geography helps students understand the physical world in which they live. It helps them see how different parts of their environment are connected and how all of those parts impact their lives and the lives of others.

Text Matters

SHORT TEXTS FOR LEARNING ABOUT COLONIAL TIMES

Kids need engaging texts and resources they can sink their teeth into. Just as with previously published *Toolkit Text* collections of articles, these articles on colonial times offer rich, engaging content that paints a vivid "big picture" of this time period. In this resource, we have included families of articles on a common topic or theme, with the understanding that the more widely kids read on a common topic, the more they learn and understand. The CCSS and other state standards expect that children will read a variety of texts on a common topic and synthesize the ideas and information.

Included here are informational articles in a number of genres: first-person accounts, plays, historical fiction, and feature articles. Images, portraits, and paintings, and all kinds of features, such as maps, charts, and timelines, provide visual interest and additional information in the articles. Primary sources, including historical speeches, images, and documents, can be found for each topic. We have also included a short bibliography of books, magazines, documentaries, and websites for investigation. We encourage you to add as many other texts and images on a topic as you can find, to bring history to life and encourage important research skills and practices.

WHY THESE SELECTIONS?

We considered the following criteria in selecting the articles, primary sources, and images:

Interest/Content Kids love to learn about the quirky, the unusual, the unexpected, and the surprises that are essential to the study of history! Here we highlight those important but often lesser-known or unrecognized perspectives and voices from the past, for example, young people, women, Native Americans, and others. These are compelling voices, and we anticipate that these articles will ignite kids' interest as they explore historical ideas and issues.

Visual literacy Visual literacy is an essential 21st-century skill, so included here are primary sources, such as historical images, paintings, and maps. Other information-filled features in the articles include diagrams, timelines, charts, and photographs, all of which encourage interpretation, analysis, and comparison across texts and images. Images also provide another entry point for students to access historical texts. You may consider projecting the color versions of the historical images or articles rich with art for students to view as one way to generate a conversation about students' background knowledge. We also use images to introduce a particular theme or concept and model interpretation and analysis. Additional historical images can be accessed on the Digital Companion Resource or through further research online.

Writing quality and accuracy When we think back to history class, we remember writing that was dull and voiceless—too often full of the generalizations and information overload common to textbook writing. To get kids excited about history and motivated to dig deeper and learn more, we searched for articles that had vibrant language and active voice. Variety makes a difference, so we include a rich assortment of nonfiction texts and visual features, as well as a bibliography of additional well-written, authentic resources.

Our knowledge of historical times and people is ever-changing as historians learn more and unearth additional artifacts and sources. Each article has been carefully vetted for accuracy by content experts and historical researchers.

Reading level/complexity Differentiation is key. Included in the collection are articles at a variety of reading levels to provide options for student practice. For example, there are shorter, more accessible articles and longer, more in-depth ones on the same or similar topics. All articles have carefully chosen images designed to enhance the content. This allows for differentiation according to students' reading proficiency levels as well as their interest levels.

We have also carefully selected primary source documents that will give students an authentic view of and unique insights into this time period. Arcane or unusual vocabulary and unfamiliar sentence structures can present significant reading challenges. We recommend building background knowledge and historical context (see Lesson 3) before digging into these authentic documents with your students. We offer strategies for approaching the reading of primary source documents with your students in Lesson 4.

Assigning a grade level to a particular text is arbitrary, especially with content-rich selections, particularly in nonfiction with all of its supportive features. We suggest you look carefully at all the articles and choose from them based on your kids' interests and tastes as well as their reading levels.

CORRELATION CHART TO SOCIAL STUDIES STRANDS

Read across the chart to determine which social studies strands are covered in each article.

Article	History	Culture	Economics	Geography	Government
Colonial America	yes	yes	yes	yes	yes
Setting Sail	yes		yes		yes
Perilous Voyage: From the Old to the New World	yes			yes	
Native Peoples of the Northeast	yes	yes	yes	yes	yes
The First Virginians	yes	yes	yes		yes
In the Beginning: English Boys in Virginia	yes	yes		yes	
Africans in Colonial America	yes		yes	yes	yes
Angelo's Story	yes	yes	yes		
Religious Freedom in Colonial America	yes	yes			yes
Elections in the Colonies	yes				yes
What to Wear?		yes			
Colonial Cures		yes			
Craftsmen, Artisans, and Tradesmen			yes		
No Ordinary Shells	yes	yes	yes		
Frontier Life	yes	yes		yes	
Making a Pomander		yes			
Let's Dry Apples		yes			
Freedom Beckons	yes				
The New World	yes			yes	
Mutiny on the Mayflower	yes				yes
An Agreement of Trust	yes	yes			yes
At Plimoth Plantation, 1627		yes	yes	yes	
Mary Rowlandson	yes	yes			
Wetamo: Indian Queen	yes	yes			yes
Phillis Wheatley: The Mother of American Poetry		yes			
The Boston Light: America's First	yes		yes		
Life in Colonial Maryland		yes	yes	yes	
Molly Bannaky	yes	yes	yes		
Butchers, Bakers, and Bonnetmakers		yes	yes		
Ben Franklin's City	yes	yes			
Pigs and Pickpockets		yes	yes		
Africans in New Amsterdam	yes	yes	yes		
Jamestown Kids		yes			
Meet Thomas and Susannah Bridges	yes	yes	yes		
"I Won't Give Up"		yes			

chart continues on page xviii

Article	History	Culture	Economics	Geography	Government
Trading Boys, Trading Cultures		yes			
A Gift of Friendship	yes	yes			
Tsenacomoco: My World	yes	yes			
On the Backs of Laborers	yes	yes	yes	yes	
Safe Haven in Florida	yes	yes	yes		
Lazy Settlers	yes	yes			
A Jamestown Murder Mystery		yes			
Ecology Detectives				yes	
Junior Interpreters Enliven Historic Area	yes	yes			

HOW TO ACCESS THE DIGITAL COMPANION RESOURCE

The Digital Companion Resource provides all of the reproducible texts, plus primary source documents, and an image bank in a full-color digital format that is ideal for projecting and group analysis. We've also included the professional journal article, "Teaching for Historical Literacy."

To access the Digital Companion Resource,

1. Go to www.heinemann.com.

2. Click on "login" to open or create your account. Enter your email address and password or click "register" to set up an account.

3. Enter keycode TTSNFCT and click register.

4. You will receive a link to download the Colonial Times Digital Companion.

You can print and project articles and images from the Digital Companion. Please note, however, that they are for personal and classroom use only, and by downloading, you are agreeing not to share the content.

These buttons are available at the top of each article for your convenience:

 will print the current article.

 will jump to the next article.

 will jump to the image bank when there are correlating images.

For best results, use Adobe Reader for Windows PC or Mac. Adobe Reader is also available as an app for iPad and Android tablets. However, the Print function will not work on tablets.

HOW MIGHT I USE THIS RESOURCE?

In the first column we summarize foundational comprehension strategies that foster student engagement and understanding across content areas, but particularly in content literacy. As students build their own repertoire of reading and thinking strategies, these become tools they use 24/7. The second column describes how students use these strategies to acquire knowledge and deepen their understanding of history.

Comprehension strategies for content literacy	Students use these in history when they:
Monitor understanding.	Stop, think, and react during reading. Learn new information and leave tracks of thinking by annotating the text. Respond to and discuss the text by asking questions, connecting to prior knowledge and experiences, drawing inferences, and considering the big ideas.
Activate and build background knowledge.	Connect the new to the known; use background knowledge to inform reading. Recognize misconceptions and be prepared to revise thinking in light of new evidence. Consider text and visual features. Pay attention to text structures and different genres.
Ask and answer questions.	Ask and answer questions to: <ul><li>Acquire information.</li><li>Investigate and do research.</li><li>Interpret and analyze information and ideas.</li><li>Read with a critical eye and a skeptical stance.</li><li>Explore lingering and essential questions.</li></ul>
Draw inferences and conclusions.	Infer ideas, themes, and issues based on text evidence. Analyze and interpret different perspectives and points of view.
Determine importance.	Sort and sift important information from interesting but less important details. Construct main ideas from supporting details. Evaluate the information and ideas in a text. Distinguish between what the reader thinks versus what the author wants the reader to understand.
Summarize and synthesize.	Analyze, compare, and contrast information across sources to build content knowledge and understanding. Evaluate claims and supporting evidence. Generate new knowledge and insights.

Adapted from Anne Goudvis and Stephanie Harvey, 2012. "Teaching for Historical Literacy." *Educational Leadership* March 2012: 52-57.

TEN CONTENT LITERACY LESSONS FOR CLOSE READING IN HISTORY

"The most obvious way to enhance students' world knowledge is to provide knowledge-enriching experiences in school; yet literacy programs have long missed the opportunity to use reading, writing, and speaking as tools for developing knowledge." (Cervetti et al., 2009)

This is especially true for history. We believe strongly that kids should be reading, writing, thinking, and doing in history. But far too often, conventional history instruction has focused on memorizing facts and dates without learning about the time period, the people themselves, and the challenges they faced. This dumbed-down approach to history is a sure way to put students to sleep and guarantee they never come to understand the discipline, much less engage in it.

In this resource, we have designed ten lessons that merge effective, foundational content-literacy practices with thoughtful approaches to reading historical articles, viewing images, and reasoning through documents. These lessons encourage thoughtful reading and discussion that go far beyond answering the questions at the end of the chapter. By teaching these ten lessons, teachers will guide students to use reading and thinking strategies as tools to acquire and actively use knowledge in history.

Lesson	Title	Page
1	Read and Annotate: Stop, think, and react using a variety of strategies to understand	L1
2	Annotate Images: Expand understanding and learning from visuals	L3
3	Build Background to Understand a Primary Source: Read and paraphrase secondary sources to create a context for a topic	L6
4	Read and Analyze a Primary Source: Focus on what you know and ask questions to clarify and explain	L9
5	Compare Perspectives: Explore the different life experiences of historical figures	L12
6	Read Critically: Consider point of view and bias	L15
7	Organize Historical Thinking: Create a question web	L18
8	Read with a Question in Mind: Focus on central ideas	L21
9	Surface Common Themes: Infer the big ideas across several texts	L24
10	Synthesize Information to Argue a Point: Use claim, evidence, and reasoning	L27

Bibliography

BOOKS ABOUT COLONIAL TIMES

Arenstam, Peter, John Kemp, Catherine O. N. Grace, Sisse Brimberg, and Cotton Coulson. *Mayflower 1620: A New Look at a Pilgrim Voyage.* Washington, D.C.: National Geographic, 2003.

Bowen, Gary. *Stranded at Plimoth Plantation, 1626.* New York: HarperCollins, 1994.

Bruchac, Joseph, and Greg Shed. *Squanto's Journey: The Story of the First Thanksgiving.* San Diego: Silver Whistle, 2000.

Foley, Sheila. *Faith Unfurled: The Pilgrims' Quest for Freedom.* Lowell, Mass.: Discovery Enterprises, 1993.

Furbee, Mary R. *Outrageous Women of Colonial America.* New York: Wiley, 2001.

Grace, Catherine O. N., Margaret M. Bruchac, Sisse Brimberg, and Cotton Coulson. *1621: A New Look at Thanksgiving.* Washington, D.C.: National Geographic Society, 2001.

Hakim, Joy. *A History of US: The First Americans: Pre-History–1600.* 3rd ed. New York: Oxford University Press, 2007.

Hakim, Joy. *A History of US: Making Thirteen Colonies: 1600–1740.* 3rd ed. New York: Oxford University Press, 2007.

Hoose, Phillip M. *We Were There, Too!: Young People in U.S. History.* New York: Farrar Straus Giroux, 2001.

Penner, Lucille R. *Eating the Plates: A Pilgrim Book of Food and Manners.* New York: Macmillan, 1991.

Plimoth Plantation Education Department. *Wampanoag: People of the East: 17th-Century Wampanoag Life.* Plymoth, MA: Plimoth Plantation, 2006.

Roop, Connie, Peter Roop, and Shelley Pritchett. *Pilgrim Voices: Our First Year in the New World.* New York: Walker and Co., 1995.

Sullivan, George. *Pocahontas.* New York: Scholastic Reference, 2001.

Waters, Kate, and Russ Kendall. *Tapenum's Day: A Wampanoag Indian Boy in Pilgrim Times.* New York: Scholastic, 1996.

Waters, Kate, and Russ Kendall. *Samuel Eaton's Day: A Day in the Life of a Pilgrim Boy.* New York: Scholastic, Inc., 1993.

Waters, Kate, and Russ Kendall. *Sarah Morton's Day: A Day in the Life of a Pilgrim Girl.* New York: Scholastic, Inc., 1989.

Weatherly, Myra. *Benjamin Banneker: American Scientific Pioneer.* Minneapolis: Compass Point Books, 2006.

DOCUMENTARIES

We Shall Remain: America Through Native Eyes. Dir. Chris Eyre, Sharon Grimberg. Perf. Benjamin Bratt, Michael Greyeyes, Marcos Akiaten, Jackson Walker. PBS, 2009. DVD.

MAGAZINES

Cobblestone, an American history magazine for grades 5–9

Dig, an archaeology and history magazine for grades 5–9

Kids Discover, a social studies and scientific magazine for grades 3–7

Junior Scholastic, a current events and social studies magazine for grades 5–8

The New York Times Upfront, a current events and social studies magazine (both national and international news) for middle and high school students

Scholastic News, a curriculum-connected current events news weekly online for grades 1–6

US Studies Weekly, a US history newspaper for students in grades K–9

WEBSITES

Library of Congress: http://www.loc.gov

Plimoth Plantation: http://www.plimoth.org/

Colonial Williamsburg: http://www.history.org/

Smithsonian Museum: http://www.si.edu/

Kids Discover: http://www.kidsdiscover.com/

PBS: http://www.pbs.org/

Works Cited

Allington, Richard L., and Peter H. Johnston. 2002. *Reading to Learn: Lessons from Exemplary Fourth-Grade Classrooms*. New York: Guilford.

Anderson, Richard C. and P. David Pearson. 1984. "A Schema-Theoretic View of Basic Processes in Reading Comprehension." In *Handbook of Reading Research*, Vol. 1. Edited by P. David Pearson, R. Barr, M.L. Kamil, and P. Mosethal, 255–291. White Plains, N.Y.: Longman.

Cervetti, Gina N., Carolyn A. Jaynes, and Elfrieda H. Hiebert. 2009. Increasing Opportunities to Acquire Knowledge through Reading. *Reading More, Reading Better*. Edited by E.H. Hiebert, Guilford Press.

Goudvis, Anne, Stephanie Harvey, Brad Buhrow, and Anne Upczak-Garcia. 2012. *Scaffolding the Comprehension Toolkit for English Language Learners*. Portsmouth, New Hampshire: Heinemann.

Goudvis, Anne, and Stephanie Harvey. 2012. "Teaching for Historical Literacy." *Educational Leadership* March 2012: 52–57.

Keene, Ellin Oliver, Susan Zimmermann, Debbie Miller, Samantha Bennett, Leslie Blauman, Chryse Hutchins, Stephanie Harvey, et al. 2011. *Comprehension Going Forward: Where We Are and What's Next*. Portsmouth, New Hampshire: Heinemann.

Pearson, P.D., Elizabeth Moje, and Cynthia Greenleaf. 2010. "Literacy and Science, Each in the Service of the Other." *Science* April 23 (328): 459–63.

President and Fellows of Harvard College. 2007. *Interrogating Texts: Six Reading Habits to Develop in Your First Year at Harvard*. Available at: http://hcl.harvard.edu/research/guides/lamont_handouts/interrogatingtexts.html.

Read and Annotate

Stop, think, and react using a variety of strategies to understand

Annotating text while reading can be a powerful thinking tool. The practice of responding to the text—paraphrasing, summarizing, commenting, questioning, making connections, and the like—actively engages the reader in thinking about the main issues and concepts in that text. The purpose of this lesson is to encourage students to leave tracks of their thinking so they better understand and remember content information and important ideas.

POSSIBLE TEXTS

The articles in this resource work for both teacher modeling and independent reading practice. Annotation is foundational practice for reading in general. Some favorites include:

- "Molly Bannaky"
- "An Agreement of Trust"
- "Setting Sail"
- "Angelo's Story"

RESOURCES & MATERIALS

- enough copies of an article for all students

CONNECT & ENGAGE

■ **Ascertain kids' prior knowledge about the text topic.**

Today we are going to read about [topic]. What do you think you know about this? Turn to someone near you and talk about [topic]. *[If the topic is unfamiliar, we project or post one or two images on the topic and allow all kids to engage in a discussion through observation and questions.]*

MODEL

■ **Show readers how to annotate thinking.**

When we annotate a text, we leave tracks of our thinking in the margins or on Post-its. I'll read a bit of the text out loud and show you my inner conversation, the thinking I do as I read. I'll annotate by taking notes to leave tracks of that thinking. These tracks allow me to look back so I can remember what I read and fully understand it. *[We read the beginning of the text out loud, stopping occasionally to ask kids to turn and talk about their own thinking and to model the following close reading strategies.]*

- Stopping to think about and react to information
- Asking questions to resolve confusion or to consider big ideas or issues
- Paraphrasing the information and jotting our learning in the margin
- Noting the big ideas or issues
- Inferring to fill in gaps in information in the text
- Bringing in prior knowledge that furthers understanding

GUIDE

■ Monitor kids' strategy use.

[After reading a paragraph or two, we turn this over to the kids by asking them to read and annotate in pairs.] Now I want you to take over jotting your thinking on your copy of the article—or on Post-its if you prefer. I'll continue reading the text and stop to let you turn, talk, and jot down your thoughts. *[As we pause in the reading, we circulate among the kids to check to see if and how they are using the strategies we modeled and if they are coming up with their own thoughts and annotations.]*

COLLABORATE/PRACTICE INDEPENDENTLY

■ Invite kids to finish the article.

Now I'll stop reading. Continue to read and annotate the article, either with a partner or on your own.

SHARE THE LEARNING

■ Invite kids to share, first in small groups and then as a class.

When you have finished the article, find two or three others who have finished. Form a group to share out your reactions to the article. Think about the important ideas in the article as well as any issues, questions, or thoughts you have. *[After groups have had time to discuss, ask kids to share out their thinking with the whole class, especially important ideas and questions.]*

FOLLOW UP

■ Kids might read related articles independently or investigate questions or gaps in information on this topic, continuing to annotate to leave tracks of their thinking.

■ Inspire kids to assume the role of historians in search of information on a particular topic, locating information online or in print, annotating their thinking as they research, and summarizing what they learned for their co-historians.

Annotate Images
Expand understanding and learning from visuals

VISUAL LITERACY IS CRITICAL TO LEARNING because graphic and pictorial elements often carry or enhance the message in print and digital media. In this lesson, we encourage close viewing and reading using a variety of entry points and aspects of visual images to gain historical information and to further understanding.

RESOURCES & MATERIALS
- a copy of an image for each student (Use the images in the text to be read as well as those from the image bank or other sources.)
- Anchor Chart with three columns headed What We Think We Know, What We Wonder, and What We Infer
- Anchor Chart: Questions to Consider When Viewing an Image

ENGAGE
■ **Invite students to study and respond to a shared image.**

[We choose one image and provide students with copies of that image or project the image for class discussion.] Look carefully at the detail in this image and really think about what you notice, infer, and wonder about it. Be sure to think about what you already know about this topic to help you understand.

■ **Chart students' thinking.**

Now turn and talk about what you know, wonder, and infer from the image. Also discuss questions and inferences that the image prompts you to think about. Keep in mind that we are always learning new information, and what we already know may be limited or even inaccurate, so be prepared to change your mind in light of new evidence. After talking, we'll come back together and share out our observations, inferences, and questions. *[We jot kids' thinking on a chart as we share out.]*

What We Think We Know	What We Wonder	What We Infer

MODEL

■ **Show students how to annotate the image with reactions, inferences, questions, and connections to prior knowledge.**

[We use kids' responses to guide our think-aloud and annotate the image with some of the important information we want them to know.] Watch me as I jot down my inner conversation about this image—those are the thoughts that go through my head as I view it. Notice the language I use to jot my thinking—and how I annotate my thoughts right on the copy of the image. I might choose a small part of the image and view it more closely.

As I look at the image, I notice … and have a strong reaction to it. I think this is about…. When I read the caption here, it tells me more about what this is. Additional text will certainly add more important information. But I respond to the image first, to get a sense of what it's all about. And I ask myself some questions: What is the purpose of this document? What's the purpose of this image? Who created it and why? I can infer the answers to these questions, and I may get them answered when I read on, but I may even need to do further research when I am finished to get a more complete understanding.

GUIDE/COLLABORATE

■ **Encourage kids to work in pairs to annotate their copies of the image.**

Now it's your turn. Choose from among the remaining images and work with a partner to discuss and record your thoughts. Annotate your copies of the image with your own ideas: what you notice, questions you have, connections to your background knowledge. You might want to look back at our original thinking about the image that we recorded on our chart. I'll come around and listen in on your conversations and post some questions you might consider as you annotate your image.

Questions to Consider When Viewing an Image

Who created this and why?

When I looked at this part of the image, I wondered….

What can we infer from this image and other features?

What can we infer from other information we viewed or read?

How do images such as this help us better understand the topic?

SHARE THE LEARNING

- Record kids' thinking as they share ideas and questions about the images.

Come back together now and let's discuss our background knowledge, questions, and inferences. *[We call kids' attention to the* What We Think We Know, What We Wonder, *and* What We Infer *chart we began earlier.]* Do we understand who created these images? Do we now understand some different perspectives on this topic? Turn and talk about how images such as these enhance our understanding of the topic. Did your thinking change after closely viewing these images and talking about them?

FOLLOW UP

- Find more images for students to choose from that are related to the topic under study. (See the table of contents for the image bank for some possibilities.) Encourage kids to work in pairs or independently to study the images closely, guided by the *Questions to Consider When Viewing an Image* chart. As kids share out what they learned from each of the images, the whole class learns from multiple images.

- What images or artifacts of today will historians of the future study to learn about us? Invite students to create a time capsule of images—personal photographs, print images, artifacts—and imagine what future historian will infer about our times.

Build Background to Understand a Primary Source
Read and paraphrase secondary sources to create a context for a topic

PRIMARY SOURCES can only be read in historical context. Just like working historians, students with background knowledge about the events, people, and ideas behind a primary source are far better able to interpret and understand it. Historians read secondary sources extensively to get a better understanding of historic events and ideas. Then they use the knowledge they have built to interpret and understand the primary source, ultimately using all sources to arrive at a more robust understanding. This lesson is preparation for Lesson 4; here, students build background knowledge by paraphrasing and getting the gist of secondary sources to prepare for study of a primary source document in Lesson 4.

RESOURCES & MATERIALS

- a copy of a primary source document or artifact to project or show
- several secondary sources related to the time period in which the primary source was created, enough copies for all students
- chart paper

ENGAGE

■ **Define primary source and surface background knowledge.**

[We briefly project a copy of a primary source document.] What you see here is a copy of what is called a *primary source.* A primary source is an original document or artifact that is created at a specific point in history by someone who lived at that time. When we read or study a primary source, it's important to have some context for it—who wrote or said or created it, why was it written or created, and what historical events surrounded it.

This primary source was created by [creator] in [time period]. Turn and talk about what you know about this time period, this person, and what was happening at the time. *[Kids share background knowledge with a partner.]* Let's come back together and share out some of your prior knowledge about this. *[We list some of the ideas and information that kids come up with on a chart for all to see.]*

Model

■ **Demonstrate how to paraphrase and annotate secondary sources to build knowledge about a topic.**

To prepare for studying this primary source, we'll be reading two articles about this person/this time period/these events. The articles are known as *secondary sources*; they are nonfiction articles written to inform us about a historical time. We'll use what we learn from reading them to inform our reading of this primary source.

As I read, I'm going to read for the essence of what's happening during this time period, with these people. My purpose is to get the gist—to capture the important events and big ideas to add to my store of knowledge. So I'm going to read a small section of the text, stop and think about it, and then write in my own words what is going on or what I learned from this section.

[We read the beginning of the text aloud.] After reading this part, I'm going to paraphrase, or put into my own words, what happened. I'll write a short phrase or two in the margin about this. Notice how I bracket this section of the text and jot down the gist as I read. From this section, I learned … and I'm thinking this will help me understand our primary source because I now have a bit of a historical context for it.

Guide

■ **Continue reading as kids paraphrase information and annotate in the margins of the text.**

Now it's your turn. I'll keep reading aloud, but I'll stop to let you turn and talk, annotate your thinking, and write down the gist of this next section of the text. Remember to focus on the most important information and ideas that you think relate to the primary source we're going to read. *[We listen in to partner talk and glance at marginal annotations to make sure kids are getting the point. We then ask kids to share out what they have learned from the reading so far.]*

Collaborate/Practice Independently

■ **Invite kids to continue reading secondary sources to build background about the time period under study.**

[We let students continue independently with the same article or—for more experienced classes—encourage them to choose among additional related secondary sources.] Keep reading about…, and continue to paraphrase and annotate in the margins as you read. Note that we don't always have to read sources word by word, but can skim and scan to find the parts that are most helpful to our purpose.

SHARE

▪ **Chart students' learning.**

Let's come together and discuss the information we found. We'll write down some of what you discovered as you read to get the gist. Remember, share out what you think will help us most with reading our primary source. I'll add to our list so we can keep this information and these ideas in mind as we read.

FOLLOW UP

▪ Read a primary source that relates to the information that students learned in this lesson. Use Lesson 4 to further support primary source reading.

▪ Challenge kids in pairs or teams to summarize—as historians might—the key information behind the topic under study and present their findings to the rest of the class in a creative, memorable format (e.g., art, diorama, poster).

4 | Read and Analyze a Primary Source

Focus on what you know and ask questions to clarify and explain

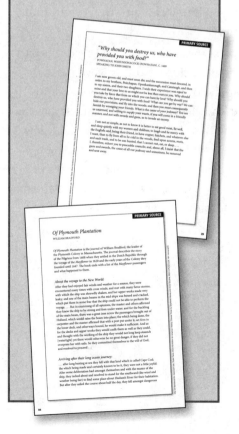

POSSIBLE TEXTS

Any reasonably accessible primary source document related to a time period or topic under study is suitable for this lesson. The following primary sources are included in this collection:

- "Why should you destroy us, who have provided you with food?" by Powhatan
- "Struggling to Settle Jamestown" by John Smith
- The Mayflower Compact
- "A Shelter for the poor and persecuted" by Roger Williams
- "Of Plimoth Plantation" by William Bradford

PRIMARY SOURCE DOCUMENTS can offer unique insights into the time period students are studying, but they often present significant reading challenges. Created in different time periods and for a variety of purposes, these documents are often characterized by unfamiliar formats, arcane language—both archaic or unusual vocabulary and unfamiliar or difficult sentence structures—and content beyond the experience of today's reader. This lesson offers a strategy for approaching the reading of primary source documents. It is important to do Lesson 3 to build a historical context before we ask kids to analyze a primary source, because students need a great deal of background knowledge about the topic at hand. We would not consider having them read a primary source cold without any knowledge of the historical context.

RESOURCES & MATERIALS

- a primary source document, enough copies for every student
- Anchor Chart: Reading Primary Source Documents

CONNECT & ENGAGE

■ Review the definition of primary source.

For a while we've been studying about [time period], right? So we already know a bit about it. One way to understand even more about that time is to read *primary source documents*. Who can remind us what a primary source is? *[We let students share their background knowledge and define primary source as "information—an original document or artifact—created at a specific point in history." They should know this from the previous lesson.]*

It's important to have a good deal of background knowledge about the people and events of the time period before tackling a complex primary source because these documents often have words and expressions that we don't use today. We call this arcane language. It's common for readers to come to an unfamiliar word or an idea and get stuck. Even if we read on to clarify understanding, reading on in a primary source sometime leads to even more confusion because there are so many unfamiliar words and concepts.

MODEL

- Explain a strategy for reading a primary source containing arcane language.

Let's take a look at this example of a primary source document. I'll read aloud the first couple of sentences. *[We read aloud enough to give kids a taste of the language.]* Wow. Pretty hard to understand, isn't it? That's why when we read primary sources we usually need to read it several times to make sense of it and get the right idea. However, just reading it over and over doesn't help. We need to read it closely and use strategies to understand what we don't know. We particularly need to think about any background knowledge we already have.

Have you ever come to a word or an idea you didn't understand when you were reading? Turn and talk about a time you remember that happening and what you did to understand what you were reading. *[Kids turn and talk and share out a few examples of ways they figured out difficult words and language.]*

One of the best ways to understand a primary source with a lot of unfamiliar words and ideas is to focus on what we *do* understand the first time we read it, perhaps think about what we have already learned about the content. Too often we get stuck on an unfamiliar word and that's it. So we focus on what we *do* understand the first time we read it and get a general idea of what the source is mostly about. Then when we reread it, we think about our questions and address those.

- Model how to write notes on what you know and questions you wonder about.

OK, so let's try it. *[We read a paragraph of the document.]* As I read this part of the document the first time, I don't have a clue what this word means, so I am not going to try to read it over and over. But I do understand this one, because I have some background knowledge about it. I can tell that the writer must have meant… when writing this. Thinking about what I know helps me get through this difficult text. So although there are quite a few words here that I do not understand, I can at least begin to get an idea of what this is mainly about by focusing on what I know. I'll also jot down any questions I have. We will get more information when we read this again.

So here is an Anchor Chart with some guidelines to help as we read primary sources. *[We review the process for each of the readings outlined on the Anchor Chart and then use the beginning of our document to model the first step. As we model, we make clear that any annotations focus on what we understand and on questioning difficult parts.]*

Reading Primary Source Documents

Reading #1: Focus on what you know. Annotate the text with what you do understand and ask questions about what you don't.

Reading #2: Use what you have come to understand to figure out the answers to your questions and infer the meaning of puzzling parts.

Successive Reading: Fill in the gaps by noting previous annotations, asking and answering questions, and making inferences for a more robust understanding.

GUIDE/PRACTICE INDEPENDENTLY

■ Monitor kids' primary source strategy use as they continue on their own.

Now work in pairs to think through this primary source document. Continue reading it with a partner, thinking about what you already know to understand new information. Annotate any important ideas you understand and write questions about the parts you need to come back to figure out. *[We circulate to make sure students can actually annotate and make progress with the text, pulling them back together to tackle it as a group if not.]*

SHARE THE LEARNING

■ Call kids together to pool their knowledge and questions.

Let's get together and share our learning and our questions. *[We go back through as much of the document as students have read, noting our understandings, answering each other's questions, and making a chart of the questions we want to figure out in the next reading.]*

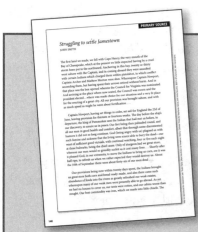

FOLLOW UP

■ The first reading of primary sources that contain particularly arcane language might take more than one session to finish. Give kids plenty of time to discuss things they understand. On subsequent readings, go back and model the process of reading for answers to questions and using known information to make inferences about the time period and the document's meaning.

■ Involve kids in a re-enactment—either dramatizing or creating a tableau—of the creation of the primary source.

Compare Perspectives

Explore the different life experiences of historical figures

POSSIBLE TEXTS

This lesson requires texts—historical fiction works particularly well—that reflect varying perspectives on the same event or time period. The following deal with the experiences of different kids in Colonial Virginia.

- "In the Beginning: English Boys in Virginia"
- "I Won't Give Up"
- "Meet Thomas and Susannah Bridges"
- "Trading Boys, Trading Cultures"
- "Jamestown Kids"
- "Tsenacomoco: My World"

WHEN WE LEARN ABOUT HISTORICAL EVENTS or a time period such as colonial times, it is important to understand that historical time from a variety of different perspectives. History is very much about the "untold stories" of people whose perspectives and experiences may not get top billing in the history books and that too often go unrecognized. But history is about all of us, so an important goal of this resource is to include voices, people, and perspectives that can provide kids with a fuller understanding of historical times and the people who lived in those times. The purpose of this lesson is to provide students with opportunities to compare and contrast life experiences of people living in the colonial time period so as to better understand their perspectives.

RESOURCES & MATERIALS

- images of different people within a particular time period
- chart paper
- a three-column chart and matching Thinksheets for each student: Person/ Experiences & Perspective/My Thinking
- articles reflecting different experiences within a particular time period

CONNECT & ENGAGE

■ **Introduce the idea of different perspectives.**

[We post images of different people of the times—children, women, and men, for example.] Let's take a look at these different people. Turn and talk about what you notice about these pictures. Who do you see? What do you think you know about some of these people? Who is not here?

Even though all these people lived at the same time, let's consider how they might have experienced life in colonial times. Who has some background knowledge or some ideas about this? *[We record kids' background knowledge and thoughts on a chart, guiding them to understand that each person pictured experiences life in a different way.]*

We're going to read a variety of different articles today and compare and contrast the lives of different people who lived in this time period. We'll consider what might be similar about peoples' lives and what might be very different. Let's read part of one account together and then you'll read another account with a different perspective with a small group.

MODEL

■ **Record text evidence reflecting a person's experiences and perspective in a historical time.**

[To prepare kids to compare and contrast different perspectives later in the lesson, we think aloud to model how to think about a historical character's experiences.] I'm going to read this historical fiction article that is written from the perspective of [person or people]. Although it is fiction, there is authentic information here that shows us what these people's lives were like.

Person	Experiences & Perspective	My Thinking

I'll begin by identifying who this is about and then read this account aloud. I'll read to find out what important experiences he/she had and how these shaped the person's perspective, or point of view. Using evidence from the text and perhaps the historical record, I'll also jot down my thinking about their experiences and point of view. I can organize my thinking on this chart:

GUIDE

■ **Guide pairs to jot down text evidence for important aspects of a person's experience.**

[We hand out a three-column Thinksheet—Person/Experiences & Perspective/ My Thinking—to each student.] Now I'll keep reading and ask you to work with someone sitting near you to ferret out more of these peoples' experiences as well as their perspectives on the times. You and your partner can discuss this and also record your thinking. Remember, the thinking column includes your interpretations and inferences as well as your questions from your reading.

COLLABORATE/PRACTICE INDEPENDENTLY

■ **Ask kids to work in small groups to study other historical characters.**

Now choose another article about a different person living in this same time period. Get together with three or four friends who are interested in the same article and record your thinking on your Thinksheets. As you read, think about how your historical characters' experiences affected their points of view, their perspectives on the times. Be sure to tie their experiences and perspectives to the text and also include your thinking.

SHARE THE LEARNING

■ Invite students to talk about their characters and compare them to others'.

[Once students have surfaced a variety of perspectives, we reconvene the group to compare and contrast the different lives of the people they read about.] Now let's talk about the historical characters in your articles. We consider how their experiences influenced their view of the world, and how people differ based on these life experiences. *[Kids love to work big, and large posters can be very helpful for sharing out the experiences/evidence information that kids have gathered.]*

Questions to guide sharing:
- What experiences did your character have?
- How did this person's experiences shape his or her perspective?
- How are his or her experiences like or different from other people we read about?
- Do you think this person's life experiences and perspective might have been, to some extent, "unrecognized" in general historical accounts of colonial times?
- Discuss why his or her perspective and life experiences are important to an understanding of people of this time period.
- Why do you think it might be important to consider a lot of different experiences and perspectives when studying history?

FOLLOW UP

■ Provide additional groups of articles organized to highlight different viewpoints and perspectives on the same time period and engage students in comparing and contrasting different views.

■ Ask students each to assume the role of a historical character they have read about. Put two or three different characters together and prompt them to discuss an event or condition of their time from the perspective of their character: What do you think about . . . ?

Read Critically
Consider point of view and bias

POSSIBLE TEXTS

This lesson is best taught with articles that have specific and clearly different points of view.

- "Mary Rowlandson"
- "Wetamo: Indian Queen"
- "Phyllis Wheatley: The Mother of American Poetry"
- "Molly Bannaky"

As we read historical sources, it is important to read with a critical eye and a skeptical stance. Some articles provide balanced, "objective" information on a topic or issue; in these, often several different perspectives and points of view are represented. Other articles may be written from a specific point of view with a definite perspective or bias. Many articles fall somewhere in between. One way to support kids to become questioning readers is to show them how to discern the purpose of the sources they read. In this lesson, we help kids surface the intent of the article's writer and discuss why it was written.

RESOURCES & MATERIALS

- Anchor Chart: Considering Point of View and Bias
- copies of two articles representing different perspectives on the same person, event, or time

CONNECT & ENGAGE

▬ **Introduce questions that explore purpose, point of view, and bias.**

[We project or share a copy of an article and discuss the title and its author. We pose questions to prompt kids to think about the point of view.] Before we read an article, it is helpful to discern whether the intent of the article is to be objective and offer information from several points of view or if it is written from a particular perspective. We ask ourselves questions like these.

Considering Point of View and Bias

- What is the author's purpose for writing the article? Is it written to inform us about a topic? To persuade us to have a particular opinion or view? For some other reason?
- Are several points of view or perspectives on the topic expressed? Or is there just one?
- What is the source of the information in the article?
- Can we detect any bias given the ideas in the article and the sources the author used to write the article?

Turn and talk about some of these questions. *[Kids do.]* This last question asks about bias. Who can tell me what bias is? *[We discuss the term* bias *and define it as "a preference or prejudice," noting that it usually refers to a point of view that doesn't recognize opposing or balanced views.]*

MODEL

▪ **Read and think aloud to uncover the author's point of view.**

[We hand out copies of an article to each student and read the beginning aloud, keeping in mind the questions posed on the chart. We think out loud about both the information and the point of view to begin to uncover the author's purpose for writing the article.] The author of this article is writing about [historical events]. Based on what's happening here, it sounds like the author has some strong feelings and a definite perspective. Now that I read on, I learn that the information we have about these events comes from [source of information]. The actual words make me think....

From the information the author includes and the sources he or she references, I'm thinking the author may be biased. That's what I think so far.

GUIDE

▪ **Guide students to read with a critical eye and a skeptical stance.**

Now I'll keep reading. While I do, keep our questions in mind *[We reference the* Considering Point of View and Bias *Anchor Chart.]* and jot notes in the margins of your copy. What's the point of view? Can you detect any bias? What does text evidence tell you about the article's purpose?

PRACTICE INDEPENDENTLY

▪ **Invite students to finish the article independently and/or read a second article with a different point of view.**

Go ahead and read the rest of the article, jotting your notes in the margins. Keep our list of questions from the chart in mind.

SHARE THE LEARNING

▪ **Listen in on small-group sharing.**

Join together with two other people and share out your thinking about the questions on the *Considering Point of View and Bias* Anchor Chart. Did you all come to the same conclusions? What are some different points of view that you noticed? Why do you think people believed the way they did? How did their personal experiences affect their point of view?

FOLLOW UP

- Provide kids with pairs or groups of articles, images, or combinations of both that depict the same event. Encourage them to compare these, focusing on the perspectives of their creators.
- Create a dramatic interpretation of a scene from the life of a particular character. Keep in mind the point of view of each character as you write the scene.

Organize Thinking
Create a question web

POSSIBLE TEXTS

This lesson works well with a few related articles with images and text that spark kids' curiosity. Consider teaching this lesson with the following articles:

- "Africans in Colonial America"
- "Safe Haven in Florida"
- "Lazy Settlers"
- "A Jamestown Murder Mystery"

KIDS' HISTORICAL THINKING often begins with their authentic questions. We encourage kids' curiosity and engagement in history by keeping a list of their questions as we find out more about a topic or time period. We add to our knowledge of the topic as we find answers and create a list of lingering questions for research and investigation. This lesson suggests ways that students can organize questions for further study.

RESOURCES & MATERIALS

- an article containing illustrations, photographs, or other images as well as text that will stimulate students' questions
- a board, chart, or projector on which to create and display a question web
- a collection of articles on a variety of related topics under study

ENGAGE

▪ **Let kids know that their own questions are the most important ones.**

Sometimes when I read about an unfamiliar topic or learn new information, I find myself asking a lot of questions. Sometimes I ask questions to help me fill in gaps in my knowledge or explain something I don't understand. Other times I wonder what might have happened if circumstances were different, so I might ask, "What if…?" or "What might have happened if…?" Sometimes my questions go unanswered and require further investigation; we call those *lingering questions*. What I do know is that our own questions really help us dig deeper into a topic and further our understanding.

MODEL

▪ **Demonstrate how viewing and reading can prompt questions.**

We're going to do some viewing and reading—and pay special attention to our questions while we do. First, let's take a look at the image in this article. What questions does it raise for you? Next, go ahead and look over the article to see what it's about. Turn and talk about your thinking. Maybe you have some background knowledge or some thoughts about this. *[Kids share out briefly.]*

I'm going to begin viewing and reading. I'm going to stop right here because I already have a question. I'm wondering…. I'll jot that down *[I write the question on one of the stems of the question web.]* and keep going. This section of the article leads me to wonder something else. *[Again the question is written on the web.]* As I think about these questions a bigger question comes to mind. I'm going to put that in the middle of what we'll call our *question web*—it's a visual map of our questions. My bigger question goes right in the middle here:

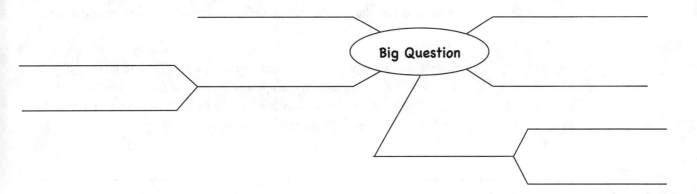

And then as I view and read, I'll add my other questions on stems around it—they are related to the big question—and put related questions near each other.

GUIDE/SHARE THE LEARNING

▪ **Read and view together, adding kids' questions to the web.**

[We read on, asking kids to turn and talk to surface their questions.] Let's keep reading and viewing together.... Let's stop here. Go ahead and turn and talk about your questions. Jot them on a Post-it so we can share them and add them to our web. *[Kids generate questions and jot these on Post-its. As they share, we have them put the questions on our group question web, guiding them to place related questions near each other.]* These are related to our big question, so we'll place them around our bigger question.

I noticed that as we kept reading, we were able to answer a couple of these questions. I can jot a short answer or response right on the web. It's just a brief thought to capture our thinking.

▪ **Share out questions that were answered as well as lingering questions.**

Now that we've finished the article, let's add any final questions to the web. Now go ahead and turn and talk with your partner and discuss if we've discovered some information that provides some insight into our big question. *[We discuss what we've learned about our big question, wrapping up the conversation by identifying lingering questions that remain.]*

COLLABORATE/PRACTICE INDEPENDENTLY

■ **Give kids a choice of investigations.**

You're going to have a choice for continuing this work. Some of you seem quite intrigued by a couple of these lingering questions—questions that remain after our reading. If you'd like, go online and see if you can find a source or two that might give you some information about your question.

Another option is to read an additional source on a topic you choose. I have a whole bunch of articles right here, so if you'd like to tackle a different article or topic, come on up and peruse these. You can work with a partner, a small group, or on your own, but be sure to pay special attention to your questions. Try organizing them on your own web.

FOLLOW UP

■ Question webs are great investigation starters. Kids often gravitate to questions and topics that matter to them, and researching answers provides the perfect opportunity for students to use their developing repertoire of reading and thinking strategies.

■ Kids love to make their thinking visible. They can create many kinds of visuals—on posters, on the computer, with a collage of images and illustrations—to share the new information they are learning.

Read with a Question in Mind
Focus on central ideas

POSSIBLE TEXTS

Articles with obvious topics that are easily identified by scanning the title and features will facilitate generation of big ideas.

- "Religious Freedom in Colonial America"
- "Elections in the Colonies"
- "No Ordinary Shells"
- "Ben Franklin's City"

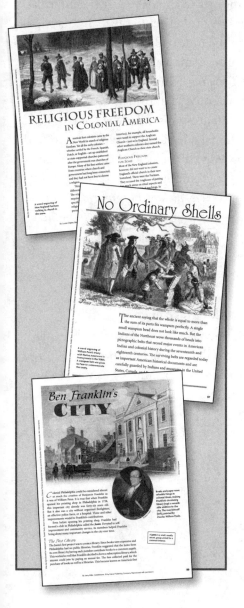

OFTEN WHEN WE READ to understand big ideas and important information, we read with a question in mind. When we keep one or two focus questions in mind as we read, we can more easily zero in on the information and ideas that are most important to understand and remember.

RESOURCES & MATERIALS

- images related to the topic currently under study, some with labels or captions, others without
- Post-it notes
- copies of an article on the topic for every student
- Anchor Chart, Reading with a Focus Question in Mind, and matching Thinksheets for every student
- a selection of additional articles on the topic

CONNECT & ENGAGE

■ **Engage students in a gallery walk.**

[We post images at different points around the room.] We have placed a variety of images around the room, all of which relate to the article we will be reading. Move around the room, look at the images, and discuss what you notice or wonder with others gathered around each image. After talking, jot down on Post-its any inferences or ideas you have about the image as well as any questions that come to mind. Stick these right on the image. You might put your initials on the Post-its you write so you can keep track of your own thinking.

MODEL

■ **Relate the kids' thoughts about the images they just observed to the topic of the article to be read. Show kids how to read with a question in mind and use a Notes/Thinking scaffold to take notes that will address the focus question(s).**

Did you guess from the pictures in your gallery walk what topic we're going to begin studying today? *[Students name the topic.]* Right! Now, let's take a quick look at this article, its title and features. What is it mostly about? Are there one or two important ideas that stand out? Turn and talk about what you were thinking and wondering about as you looked at the images in our gallery walk. How do your questions and inferences relate to the topic of the article?

- **Demonstrate how to turn the big idea of the article into a question—one that gets at the big ideas in the article.**

So, from the images and a quick look at the text, I'd guess that one of the big ideas that is important to understanding this time in history is…. I can turn this big idea into a focus question and ask…. Keeping a focus question like this one in mind will guide us to find out important information about the topic.

[We hand out the Thinksheets and call attention to the matching Anchor Chart.] To keep my thoughts organized, I'm going to write our question(s) at the top of my *Reading with a Focus Question in Mind* page. It has two columns, *Notes* and *Thinking*, because both the information from the article and our thinking about it are important!

Listen and watch as I read and take notes on the article. I'll make sure the information I record relates to the focus question. So in the *Notes* column, I'll write facts and information about our question(s); in the *Thinking* column, I'll jot down what I think about the information—my reactions and responses. Maybe I'll have some additional questions or some background knowledge, all of which I can jot in the *Thinking* column. *[We read the beginning of the article, picking out information that relates to our question, writing it on the chart, and recording our responses.]*

Reading with a Focus Question in Mind

Focus Question: _____

_____

Title: _____

Notes	Thinking

GUIDE

- **Continue to read the article aloud as kids take notes.**

Now I'll keep reading this article while you take notes. Be sure to keep the focus question(s) in mind, jotting down only information that will help you understand the answers. Remember, including our thinking as we take notes means we'll process and understand the information more thoroughly. *[We continue reading, stopping occasionally to give kids time to turn and talk about the focus question before recording their ideas on the Thinksheet.]*

COLLABORATE/PRACTICE INDEPENDENTLY

■ Give kids an opportunity to study related sources, taking notes on and responding to the focus question.

On your own or with a partner, finish reading this article and writing down your notes and thinking about this article. Next, choose one of these other articles or images and continue to think about our focus question. *[We call attention to the images posted for our gallery walk as well as a collection of related articles.]* Does this new source add to your knowledge on this topic? Read it with the focus question in mind and take notes on it.

SHARE THE LEARNING

■ Ask kids to discuss the focus question in small groups, summarizing their learning.

[We help kids form groups of three or four, making sure that among the members of the group, they have read several of the articles so they can discuss each knowledgeably.] Let's get into groups to discuss what we have learned about our focus question. Get together with two or three other people; make sure that together you have read and taken notes on several articles and images. Share with your group your learning and thinking about the articles you have read.

After you discuss the focus question using each article, take a look at the questions and inferences you jotted on the images at the beginning of the lesson. How has your thinking changed? What do you know now that you didn't when you first viewed the images? What questions that you asked still linger?

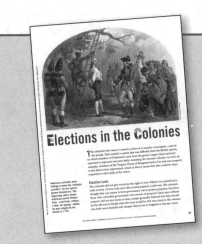

FOLLOW UP

■ In small groups, have students do follow-up research to try to resolve any lingering questions. There are many websites rich with historical information; check out the recommended resource list on page xxii to get started. If their queries are still unanswered, students might try contacting historical museums or other institutions. Researchers are often willing to answer questions, especially those of engaged, curious students.

■ Kids love to share their new findings. They can give presentations or create short movies to share the new information they are learning.

9 | Surface Common Themes
Infer the big ideas across several texts

POSSIBLE TEXTS

Any group of articles on the same historical topic will work for this lesson. A few suggestions are:

- "Africans in New Amsterdam" and "Africans in Colonial America"
- "On the Backs of Laborers" and "Life in Colonial Maryland"

IN REAL-WORLD READING, we rarely read simply one text on a topic. Generally, we read a wide range of texts on a common theme to learn more about it and to understand a variety of perspectives. We infer the big ideas across these various texts to learn more about the overall topic or issue. The purpose of this lesson is to guide students to use evidence from several texts to infer broad historical themes.

RESOURCES & MATERIALS

- two-column Anchor Chart—Evidence from the Text/Big Ideas—and matching Thinksheets for each student
- a set of resources (e.g., an expository article, a piece of historical fiction, and an image) on the same historical topic for each group of three students

CONNECT & ENGAGE

▪ **Engage the kids and review what it means to infer.**

Today we're going to interact with several texts on a single topic to get more information. The more texts we read and the more images we view, the more we learn. To better understand the issues and information, we're going to infer the big ideas across several of these texts. Does anyone remember what it means to infer? Turn and talk about that. *[Kids turn and talk and share out some thoughts.]*

Inferring is the strategy we use to figure out information that is not explicitly stated in the text. To infer the big ideas, we need to think about what we already know and then merge our background knowledge with clues in the text to make a reasonable inference and surface some big ideas or themes about the topic or issue. If our inference doesn't seem reasonable, we can gather more clues and information from the text. If we ignore text clues and rely solely on our background knowledge, our inferences could be off the mark. So we're constantly looking for clues, text evidence, and more information to make reasonable inferences and come up with big ideas. Reading a number of articles gives us more background knowledge, which gives us more information upon which to base our inferences.

MODEL

■ **Model how to use text evidence to infer big ideas.**

[We display a two-column chart on which to record evidence and big ideas.] While I'm reading this article, I'll closely read the words, and I'll pay attention to the images and features, searching for clues to help me infer the big ideas. When I find some evidence that supports a big idea, I'll write it on the chart. We can find evidence for big ideas in words, pictures, features, actions, and details that are included in the text. Usually, there are several big ideas that bubble to the surface in an article.

Evidence from the Text (words, pictures, features, actions, details)	Big Ideas

[We read the article aloud, stopping when a big idea or theme is apparent.] I think these words are good evidence for the big idea of…. So I'll write the words from the text in the *Evidence* column and the big ideas that I infer in the *Big Ideas* column. Here, these images help me to infer the big idea of…, so I'll record information about the images in the *Evidence* column, too. Sometimes I look closely at the character's actions in historical fiction to infer the big ideas. My background knowledge may be helpful here. All of these clues are evidence for the theme of….

GUIDE

■ **Invite kids to come up with text evidence for some big ideas.**

OK, now it's your turn. Let's read a bit together before you go off and try this in a small group. *[We read through a page of text.]* Now that I have read a page, turn and talk about what you think are some of the big ideas here. Look for clues and cite that as evidence for your big ideas. *[Kids share their ideas with a partner.]*

Who has a big idea they would like to share? What is the evidence for that idea?

Let's add to our chart. Sometimes the evidence came from words quoted directly from the text, and other times from pictures and features in the text.

COLLABORATE

■ **Support kids as they infer big ideas across several texts.**

Now you can get together in groups of three. I have three pieces of text; they are all different, but they focus on the same topic. Since they are grouped around a common topic, they are likely to have some similar big ideas, and all will likely include evidence for those big ideas. As you read through these articles, they will add to your background knowledge, increasing the likelihood that you will make reasonable inferences when you are inferring the big ideas. Share your thinking with each other; note the text clues and the big ideas that occur to you based on your reading and viewing and jot them on your Thinksheets. *[We distribute three related resources to each group and* Evidence from the Text/Big Ideas *Thinksheets to each student.]*

SHARE

■ **Record kids' evidence and big ideas.**

[We gather kids in a sharing session to talk about their group's big ideas and evidence.] What are some of the big ideas you inferred as you read and viewed? As you share them, I'll add them to the class's *Evidence from the Text/Big Ideas* Anchor Chart.

Did you find some similar ideas across all of the articles and images?

Great thinking about using text evidence to infer the big ideas. We can continue to make inferences beyond the book, especially if there is some good evidence to support them.

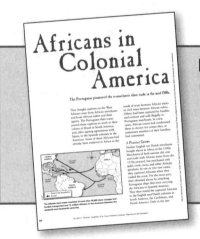

FOLLOW UP

■ Add related resources to the original three and have kids continue to look for corroboration of their big ideas—or for new ones.
■ Students might create dramatic tableaux to support their inferred themes: a series of frozen scenes carefully crafted to represent evidence of the big ideas.

10 Synthesize Information to Argue a Point
Use claim, evidence, and reasoning

A GOOD ARGUMENT expresses a point of view, uses information as evidence to support that view, and applies the information to persuade others. To make a good argument, the learner must turn information into knowledge, gathering evidence about the ideas in the text and synthesizing that information to make a claim that will convince others of the validity of the argument. To make a valid claim, however, the arguer must have some background about the issue; before making a claim and sharing the evidence, the claimant needs to have viewed or read several sources on the topic so that he or she knows enough to make a reasonable claim about it. As a result, this lesson on synthesizing information to argue a point is best taught near the end of a unit of study.

RESOURCES & MATERIALS

- several articles on the same topics or with similar themes (some read beforehand)
- three-column Anchor Chart with columns headed Claim, Evidence, and Reasoning and matching Thinksheets for each student
- Anchor Chart: Questions to Guide Effective Arguments

CONNECT & ENGAGE

■ **Invite students to share what they already know about argument.**

How many of you have ever heard the word *argument*? Turn to each other and talk about what you know about arguing. *[Kids turn and talk, then share out, mostly about personal disagreements they have had with others.]* Today we're going to talk about a more formal kind of argument.

■ **Define the term argument.**

Have you ever believed in something so much that you have wanted to convince others to agree with you? It is common to feel that way. Sometimes it happens outside when we want to make rules for a new game. Sometimes it happens at home when we are trying to get one more dessert out of Mom. And sometimes it gets a little unpleasant, with people getting mad at each other. Well, the type of argument we are talking about today is about convincing others to see the issue from your point of view. But rather than getting mad and fighting about it, in this kind of argument we gather evidence to make a point and try to convince the other side based on valid information.

So writers make arguments all the time, and they do it without fighting. They share evidence that helps them make their case. They might argue that we should eat healthier foods and support their argument with statistics showing the health risks of eating junk food. Or they might argue that soccer is a safer game than football, and to make their case share information about the danger of concussions that come from getting tackled in football. This kind of argument is based on a claim—that we should eat healthier food or that soccer is a safer game, for example. Turn to each other and talk about something you believe and would like to make a case for or a claim about. Share evidence that would back up your case. *[Kids turn and talk and then share out.]*

MODEL

■ **Read through a piece of text and show students how to use text evidence and reasoning to make and support a claim.**

When we make a claim, we need to provide evidence in support of the claim, valid evidence from a text or other source. And to make a decent argument, we need to know quite a bit about our topic. So we read about the issue or topic a bit and form an opinion. Then we merge the evidence in the text with what we already know to convince others of our claim. So let me show you how it works as I read through this article on. . . . I have an Anchor Chart here with columns headed *Claim, Evidence,* and *Reasoning.* As I read through the article, I'll collect evidence for the claim I'm making and add it to the first column.

Claim	Evidence	Reasoning

I have read a bit on this topic over the past week or so, and I already have a belief or opinion about it that I can turn into a claim. I'll state my claim—that is, the argument that I am going to try to make about the issue—in the first column. *[We write a claim in the first column and continue reading.]*

Here is some evidence for my claim. … supports my claim because…. I'll jot this in the second column.

Now in the third column, I'm going to show my reasoning—how I interpret the evidence to support my claim. I believe . . . because the evidence shows me that. . . .

It helps that I have learned about this topic beforehand. I already knew … from previous readings, so I can reasonably make this claim based on the evidence from this article as well as from my background knowledge.

Reasoning is an important part of this process because if my goal is to make a case for my point of view and convince others, I need to be able to reason through this issue or topic myself in order to understand it well enough to persuade others. And always remember, an argument is not just our opinion, but our point of view supported by evidence.

GUIDE/COLLABORATE

▪ **Encourage students to work in pairs to read through an article, make a claim, and support it with evidence and reasoning.**

So it's time for you to give it a whirl. With partners, choose one of these articles on [the same topic or issue]. Talk about what you already know about the topic based on the article we just read together as well as other things you've learned. Think about an argument, or claim, you would like to make. Write your claim on your Thinksheet. As you read this additional article, look for evidence that supports your claim and jot that down as well. And talk with your partner about your reasoning.

Think about some of these questions as you reason through the text. *[We display guiding questions and read them aloud.]*

Go ahead and get started. I'll come around and check in with your partnerships as you reason through the text, thinking about your claim and the evidence you find to support it. Remember, if you can't find evidence to fit your claim, you might need to revise your claim to fit the evidence!

Questions to Guide Effective Arguments

- What is my point?
- Who is my audience?
- What might the audience already think about this argument?
- Does the evidence back up my claim? If so, how?
- Which evidence will most likely convince my audience of my claim?
- What would be a good counterargument? Is there evidence to support the other side? If so, what is it?

SHARE

▪ **Bring kids back together to share their claims, evidence, and reasoning.**

[Kids share their forms and we discuss their claims as well as possible counterarguments.] Whenever we make an argument, we need to be prepared for a counterargument—a claim that contradicts our own. When faced with an opposite opinion, we need to address it with more evidence in support of our own claim or with evidence that disproves the opposite claim.

FOLLOW UP

- This is an introductory lesson on synthesizing information to present an argument. Since making an effective case is a complex process, it requires repeated discussions and practice. So teaching this lesson with a wide variety of issues and articles comprises the next steps.

- Teaching kids to write a paper with a strong argument is an eventual goal. A good resource to support that process is available at the University of North Carolina Writing Center http://writingcenter.unc.edu/handouts/argument. This site will support you as you engage kids in claim-and-evidence writing, although it needs to be adapted for kids younger than college age.

Colonial AMERICA

IF YOU LIVED IN COLONIAL AMERICA—the period from the first colonies to the American Revolution—then you might have been alive during a time of great change. Of course, your perspective depended on who you were, where you were living, and what you did. Native Americans, European settlers, and enslaved Africans and indentured servants all experienced this time of change differently.

If you were one of the native peoples who lived in America before the settlers arrived, you would witness almost everything about your world changing, and not usually for the best. The Native Americans' lifestyles were completely different from those of the Europeans who began to settle in their area. There were many different tribes, each with its own language and way of life that was suited to their homeland. All tribes had a deep respect for the land; tribes hunted, fished, and gathered fruits, as well as farming the fertile lands on which they lived. When the Europeans arrived, they brought with them new ideas about owning land and farming, which were not compatible with the way that natives had been living their lives for hundreds of years. Although different Native Americans tribes inhabited certain areas, most Native American cultures did not believe in the permanent land ownership. On the other hand, Europeans came from a tradition of individually owned land and property.

As the colonists settled on the lands once inhabited only by Native Americans, they traded with them. Natives traded corn and furs for colonial cloth or things made of iron. Some tribes established treaties with the newcomers and lived together peacefully

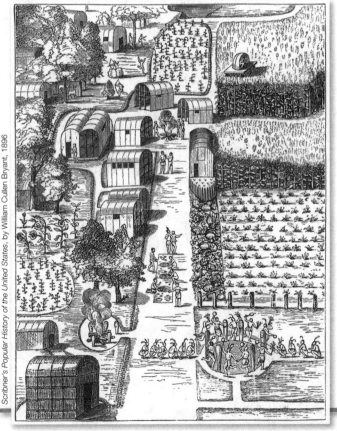

Scribner's Popular History of the United States, by William Cullen Bryant, 1896

An engraving of an Algonquin village, Secotan.

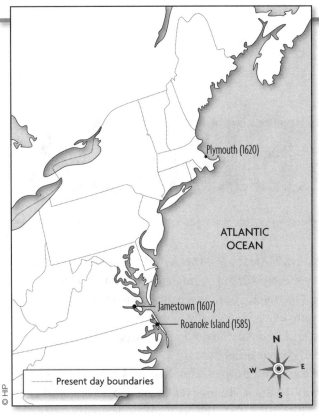

Map showing the English Colonies.

for many years. But as more settlers came to the 13 colonies, they used natural resources that Native Americans depended on for food, and claimed native land. This led to times of strife, such as King Philip's War. We can learn about these times from the Native American female leader, or sachem, Queen Wetamo, and the white colonist Mary Rowlandson, who was captured by Native Americans. Eventually Native Americans had little choice except to move west to places where white settlers had not yet settled.

If you were a settler who lived in the original 13 colonies, chances are that you came there from England, or that your parents were English. The first settlers at Jamestown in 1607 were English. They came because they were hoping to get rich, after hearing stories of the Spanish explorers finding gold in South America, but the harsh environment of the New World nearly killed them. In 1620, another group of settlers arrived in America. The Pilgrims were not looking for riches. They just wanted to be able to practice their religion without being persecuted. The Puritans followed the Pilgrims ten years later, also seeking to establish a new church. Religious freedom was the reason

New England Puritans walking to church in the snow.

Slaves unload rice barges in South Carolina.

why Quakers settled in Pennsylvania. There was even a colony (Maryland) established for English people who were in legal trouble for not paying their debts. Some of the new residents of the colonies were indentured servants, who agreed to work for certain number of years, usually seven, to pay for their passage to the new world. After their indenture period was up, they were free.

While half of the people who settled in the colonies could trace their heritage directly back to England, the next largest group actually came from Africa. As early as the mid-1500s, the Portuguese were capturing Africans and selling them as slaves to the Spanish to work in their colonies in the Americas. The first slaves to be sold directly to the American colonies came to Jamestown in 1619. After that, the number of slaves brought from Africa or the Caribbean increased every year. Enslaved people in the New England colonies often performed household duties and skilled labor, working as carpenters, blacksmiths, bakers, and weavers. In the southern colonies, some slaves performed these same household duties, but many more worked in the tobacco fields. They often brought the knowledge of how to cultivate rice and tobacco with them from their native lands. At first they often worked and lived side by side with indentured servants. But towards the end of the 1600s, slaves gradually began to live in their own quarters, which were like small villages. Unlike indentured servants, they were unable to work their way to freedom.

Life differed depending on where in the 13 colonies you lived. Over time, cities such as Boston, Philadelphia and New York had established populations, but most people lived in scattered settlements on farms and small towns. New Hampshire, Massachusetts, Rhode Island and Connecticut had rich forests for timber, good fishing, and plenty of game for trapping. This made it easy for them to trade goods with Europe. Farming was not very good because of the rocky soil and the number of trees, and most families only grew enough food to feed themselves. The Middle Colonies (New York, New Jersey, Pennsylvania, and Delaware) had both excellent farming and good harbors for shipping. Farmers grew grain and raised livestock, and traded these raw materials for manufactured goods from Europe. The Southern colonies, including Maryland, Virginia, North Carolina, South Carolina, and Georgia, grew both their own food and crops to trade, such as tobacco, rice, and indigo. Growing these kinds of crops required a lot of work and effort, so plantation owners relied on both slaves and indentured servants for labor. And no matter where you lived, there were artisans and tradesmen who created the goods that everyone needed, from candles to barrels to pewter, or provided services like doctors, wigmakers, and millers.

In Colonial America, people from many different places and cultures, including native peoples, Europeans, and Africans, had to learn how to get along with each other and ultimately build a new country. There would be many growing pains on the way to becoming the United States, and while there was discovery and excitement, there was also tragedy and heartbreak. But even today, hundreds of years later, we can still read what Colonial Americans wrote and hear their voices. Some of them we remember well, while the stories of others have been mostly hidden by history. People who lived in Colonial America were a diverse group with different perspectives, ideals, and values, really not so different from us today.

New Hampshire
Massachusetts
New York
Rhode Island
Connecticut
Pennsylvania
New Jersey
Delaware
Maryland
Virginia
North Carolina
South Carolina
Georgia

ATLANTIC
OCEAN

New England Colonies
Middle Colonies
Southern Colonies
Present day boundaries

© HIP

Map showing the
Thirteen Colonies.

COLONIAL AMERICA TIMELINE

1607

The Jamestown Colony is founded in Virginia.

A pen & ink drawing of Jamestown.

1609

Henry Hudson explores the Hudson River in New York, tobacco is first planted and harvested by Virginia colonists.

1619

The first Africans are brought to Jamestown for sale as indentured servants.

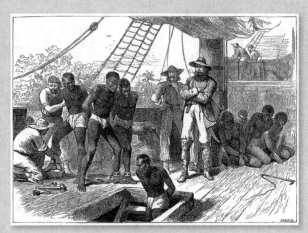

Enslaved people being loaded onto a ship.

1620

The Pilgrims arrive in Massachusetts.

1624

Thirty Dutch families arrive to establish a colony in New York.

1630

900 Puritans arrive to set up a colony in Massachusetts Bay, which becomes the city of Boston.

1634

The first settlers arrive in Maryland.

1636

The colony of Rhode Island is founded as a place for those escaping religious intolerance in Massachusetts.

Roger Williams meeting the Narragansett Indians after being banished from Massachusetts Bay Colony.

1652

Rhode Island enacts the first colonial law making slavery illegal.

1663

King Charles II of England establishes the colony of Carolina.

Left, top: © HIP. Left bottom: © Photos.com/Jupiterimages/Getty Images/HIP. Right: Picture Collection, The New York Public Library, Astor, Lenox and Tilden Foundations.

1664

The Dutch city of New Amsterdam becomes New York when it is ceded to the English.

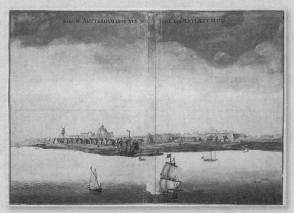

Gezicht op Nieuw Amsterdam by Johannes Vingboons, a 1664 painting of Nieuw Amsterdam.

1675–1676

King Philip's war is fought between New England colonists and Native Americans over colonial expansion into native territory.

Metacomet (called King Philip by the colonists) was the chief, or sachem, of the Wampanoag Indians in New England.

1681

Quakers found Pennsylvania.

1682

French explorer La Salle claims the lower Mississippi valley for France, naming it Louisiana.

1692

The Salem Witch trials take place in Salem, Massachusetts.

1700

The white population in the American colonies reaches 250,000 people.

1706

Benjamin Franklin is born in Boston.

Benjamin Franklin, in a painting by Charles Willson Peale.

1712

The Carolina colony is divided into North and South Carolina. Pennsylvania bans the import of slaves into its colony.

1725

The population of black slaves in the American Colonies reaches 75,000.

1731

The first public library in America is founded.

1737

The first colonial copper coins are minted in Connecticut.

1754

The French and Indian War begins.

Sir Walter Raleigh tried without luck to establish an English colony in the New World.

Setting SAIL

Sir Walter Raleigh, military adventurer and friend of England's Queen Elizabeth I, watched as the crowds cheered for Sir Francis Drake in 1580. Drake was the first Englishman to sail around the world. His ship, the *Golden Hind*, had returned filled with the silver and gold he had ***plundered*** from Spanish ships and settlements.

> **Plundered** means robbed of goods by force.
>
> **Privateers** are commanders of ships that are privately manned and owned but authorized by a government to attack and capture enemy vessels.

FAST FACT
QUEEN ELIZABETH I WAS KNOWN AS THE VIRGIN QUEEN BECAUSE SHE NEVER MARRIED.

At the time, Spain and Portugal were the most powerful nations in the western world. Their warships ruled the seas, protected their Central and South American colonies, and battled British *privateers* such as Drake.

But Raleigh knew that if England wanted to become a world power, it needed more than Spanish metals and jewels — England needed colonies of its own. Colonies could produce goods and offer safe harbors for British ships, not to mention riches for those who established settlements.

The First English Colony
The first colonizing attempt by the English in 1583 ended with ships wrecked in the stormy North Atlantic Ocean. The following year, Raleigh sent two ships from England that landed on an island off the coast of present-day North Carolina. The native people there seemed friendly, and they had furs, skins, dyes, timber, and freshwater pearls to trade. Raleigh named the new land "Virginia" in honor of England's "Virgin Queen." This new colony was much larger than the present-day state of Virginia.

Within another year, seven more ships, led by Raleigh's cousin Sir Richard Grenville, sailed from England for Virginia. Most of these colonists were soldiers and craftsmen. A scientist, Thomas Hariot (also spelled Harriot), and a mapmaker and artist, John White, also sailed.

By Linda Roberts, *Cobblestone*, © by Carus Publishing Company. Reproduced with permission.
May be reproduced for classroom use. *Toolkit Texts: Short Nonfiction for American History, Colonial Times*
by Stephanie Harvey and Anne Goudvis, ©2014 (Portsmouth, NH: Heinemann).

John White, who later became governor of the ill-fated English colony on Roanoke Island, drew this map of Virginia in about 1585.

Near land, one of the seven vessels struck a sandbar and nearly sank, losing the colonists' supply of winter food. Once on land, when an Indian stole a silver cup from the colonists, Grenville retaliated by burning down an entire Indian village. With little food and having made enemies of the native people, the colonists moved to Roanoke Island, where they could protect themselves better. Grenville sailed for England to fetch more supplies.

From New Discoveries to Harsh Realities

While the colonists waited for Grenville's return, Hariot collected plant and animal specimens, and White sketched scenes of their new environment. Together, they mapped the area. By winter, though, the colonists were hungry. When the Indians lost interest in trading food for goods, the soldiers began making demands, which turned into threats.

By June 1586, the starving men were at war with the Indians. They were saved by the sudden appearance of Drake. They sailed back to England with him, leaving no one to greet the puzzled Grenville when he returned to Virginia in August. Grenville left 15 of his men to "hold" the colony, and he, too, went back home to England.

Disappointed, Raleigh tried again the next year. In July 1587, three ships carrying about 115 craftsmen and farmers landed on Roanoke Island. They found only one skeleton from the 15 men left by Grenville. And unfortunately, the new arrivals did not fare much better. Their **pilot**, who may have been working for the Spanish, abandoned the colonists. Within six months, nearly a third of those Englishmen were dead.

White also was a member of this group. Named governor by the surviving colonists, White was chosen to go in the remaining ship to obtain help. Because White had a daughter

By Linda Roberts, *Cobblestone*, © by Carus Publishing Company. Reproduced with permission. May be reproduced for classroom use. *Toolkit Texts: Short Nonfiction for American History, Colonial Times* by Stephanie Harvey and Anne Goudvis, ©2014 (Portsmouth, NH: Heinemann).

and granddaughter at the colony, the settlers knew he would return as quickly as possible. But back in England, White found that the country was preparing for war with Spain and unable to spare ships.

A Mysterious Demise

Three years passed before the despairing White could return to Roanoke Island, and when he did, the colonists had vanished. The only evidence to indicate where they might have gone was the word "Croatoan" carved on a gatepost. But before White could sail to this nearby island inhabited by friendly Indians, a storm forced his ships far off the coast. His captain insisted on

" . . . and no one from the 'lost colony' ever was seen again."

returning to England, and no one from the "lost colony" ever was seen again.

When Queen Elizabeth died in 1603, James VI of Scotland succeeded her as King James I of England. Soon after, he accused Raleigh of *treason*, for which Raleigh eventually was beheaded. Although Virginia did not provide him with a fortune, Raleigh is remembered as the man who first settled North America for England. And the next attempt to colonize the New World by the English would be a success. Named for the new king, it was called Jamestown.

A **pilot** means one who does not belong to a ship's company but who is licensed to conduct a ship into and out of port.

Treason is the violation of allegiance toward one's country.

FAST FACT

JOHN WHITE'S DAUGHTER, ELEANOR DARE, GAVE BIRTH TO A BABY NAMED VIRGINIA SHORTLY BEFORE HE LEFT ROANOKE ISLAND. VIRGINIA WAS THE FIRST ENGLISH CHILD BORN IN AMERICA.

When rescuers returned to Roanoke Island, the settlers there had vanished, leaving only a single clue to their whereabouts: the word *Croatoan*, the name of a nearby island.

North Wind Picture Archives

By Linda Roberts, *Cobblestone*, © by Carus Publishing Company. Reproduced with permission. May be reproduced for classroom use. *Toolkit Texts: Short Nonfiction for American History, Colonial Times* by Stephanie Harvey and Anne Goudvis, ©2014 (Portsmouth, NH: Heinemann).

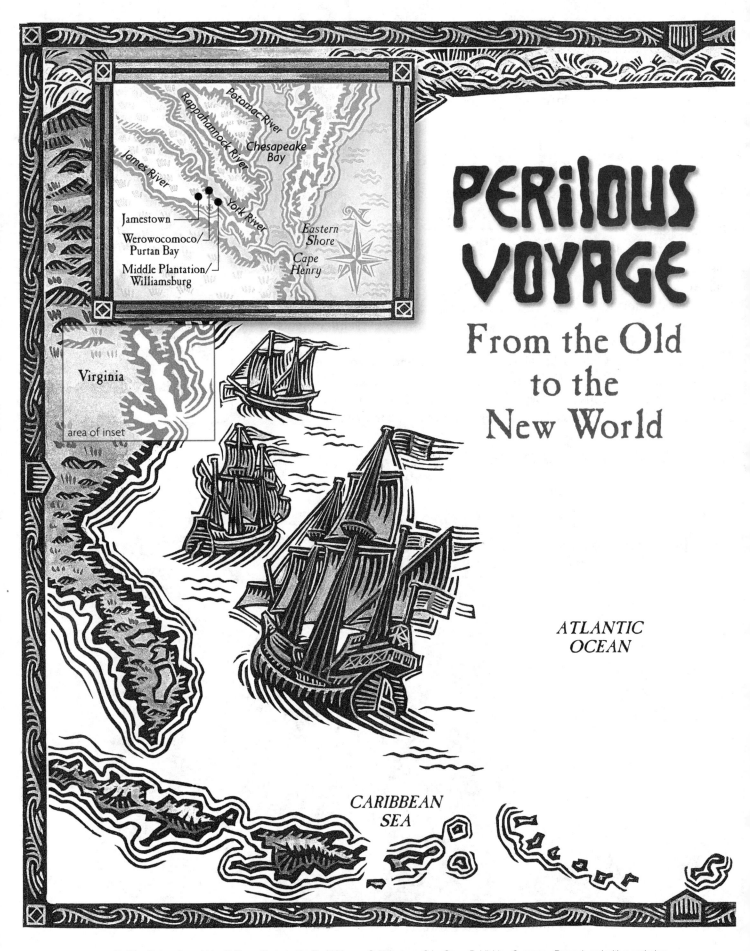

PERILOUS VOYAGE

From the Old to the New World

Potomac River

Rappahannock River

Chesapeake Bay

James River

York River

Jamestown

Werowocomoco/ Purtan Bay

Middle Plantation/ Williamsburg

Eastern Shore

Cape Henry

Virginia

area of inset

ATLANTIC OCEAN

CARIBBEAN SEA

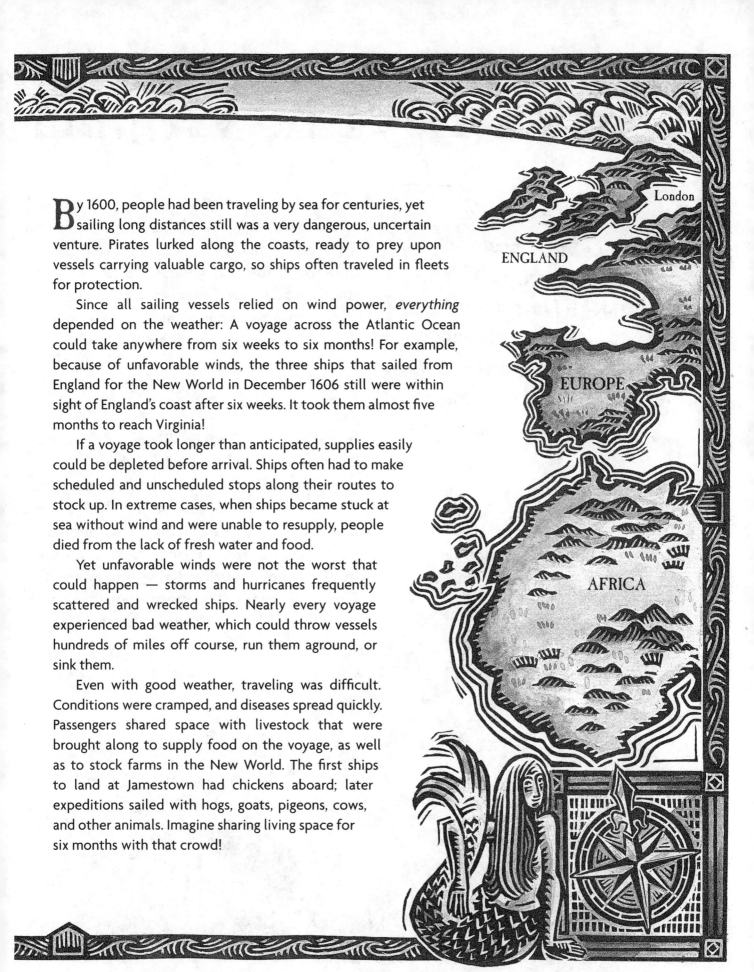

By 1600, people had been traveling by sea for centuries, yet sailing long distances still was a very dangerous, uncertain venture. Pirates lurked along the coasts, ready to prey upon vessels carrying valuable cargo, so ships often traveled in fleets for protection.

Since all sailing vessels relied on wind power, *everything* depended on the weather: A voyage across the Atlantic Ocean could take anywhere from six weeks to six months! For example, because of unfavorable winds, the three ships that sailed from England for the New World in December 1606 still were within sight of England's coast after six weeks. It took them almost five months to reach Virginia!

If a voyage took longer than anticipated, supplies easily could be depleted before arrival. Ships often had to make scheduled and unscheduled stops along their routes to stock up. In extreme cases, when ships became stuck at sea without wind and were unable to resupply, people died from the lack of fresh water and food.

Yet unfavorable winds were not the worst that could happen — storms and hurricanes frequently scattered and wrecked ships. Nearly every voyage experienced bad weather, which could throw vessels hundreds of miles off course, run them aground, or sink them.

Even with good weather, traveling was difficult. Conditions were cramped, and diseases spread quickly. Passengers shared space with livestock that were brought along to supply food on the voyage, as well as to stock farms in the New World. The first ships to land at Jamestown had chickens aboard; later expeditions sailed with hogs, goats, pigeons, cows, and other animals. Imagine sharing living space for six months with that crowd!

IN THE BEGINNING:
English Boys in Virginia

What was it like to live in Jamestown in the beginning? Read what three of the young colonists might have said about growing up along with the new colony.

December 20, 1606 "Farewell, London! We are Virginia bound! My thoughts flood with sailors' tales: rivers of gold, trees so tall they touch the sky, winds able to tear ships apart, and dangerous Indians.

My master, Captain John Smith, reminds me that I shall soon see what is and is not true. He's a good man to serve, I think. I'm a lucky lad!"

—Sam Collier

January 23, 1607 "Doomed we are! Poor weather has stalled our three ships in the Channel for weeks! My stomach turns inside out with every storm. The Susan Constant is the size of a small farmhouse—with 71 passengers and crew crammed in. (I cannot imagine living on either the Godspeed or the Discovery—both are much smaller!) We are 105 colonists (including we boys) on the three ships.

—Nathaniel Peacock

April 26, 1607 "The savages attacked us our first night in Virginia! Two of our men were wounded, but we shan't be chased from these sandy beaches and tall, strong trees. I may be a boy, but I'll fight like a man!

The Canary Islands and West Indies were happy sights. I was glad to refresh our stores with clear water, fruit, tortoises, and wild boar meat—but am gladder still to be in Virginia at last! Master Brookes died—Master Percy says the heat boiled the fat within him. I wish he could have seen this place—savages and all. Mayhaps we'll be the first to find a water route across the continent as well as be the first Englishmen to build a lasting settlement. Hurrah! I am ready!"

—*Richard Mutton*

> The English often called the native people "savages" because they did not live according to English customs. The English believed that their own ways of dressing and living and believing were the right ways. For the most part, they did not value the Virginia Native Americans' ways.

April 29, 1607 "Erected a cross at Cape Henry today, claiming Virginia for England! Captain Newport opened the sealed box with our instructions and the names of our governing council—five men plus Captain Smith. The others don't like Captain Smith. He disagrees with them. On the voyage, he was arrested for mutiny—and now he is named a leader! Newport won't let Smith on the council for now. Knowing Captain Smith, I trust that will change."

—*Sam Collier*

By Leigh Anderson, illustrated by Craig Spearing, *Appleseeds*, © by Carus Publishing Company. Reproduced with permission. May be reproduced for classroom use. *Toolkit Texts: Short Nonfiction for American History, Colonial Times* by Stephanie Harvey and Anne Goudvis, ©2014 (Portsmouth, NH: Heinemann).

May 13, 1607 "Explored the river we've named for King James and feasted with friendlier natives. The land here is sweet—clear water, large strawberries, and pearled oysters!

Discovered a peninsula today where the ships can pull close to shore. 'Twill be safer with the ships nearby. We'll build our settlement here."

—*Richard Mutton*

June 22, 1607 "James Fort is almost finished. Our tents are safe now in a triangle of upended logs. The savages struck us while Newport, Smith, and a party of men were exploring the James River. Seventeen were wounded, and one of us boys was killed!

As we built the fort and filled the ships' holds with clapboard and sassafras roots, the natives kept attacking us—sneaking up in the tall grass. Someone had the idea that we cut the grass short. Things are quieter now.

Captain Newport sailed for England today. He left the Discovery here and promises to come back with supplies."

—*Nathaniel Peacock*

January 2, 1608 "Our days are filled with guard duty, building huts, exploring, some hunting, and gathering firewood. We've not enough laborers. Some gentlemen are used to servants and refuse to work. Many have died from sickness. I'm tired and hungry: only one cup of gruel each day! But I must labor. Again and again, Captain Smith has traded with savages for beans and corn. Last month, he was captured, nearly killed, and then released by Powhatan, the local chief.

Newport's ships sighted today. There are only 38 of us left."

—Sam Collier

"SLIME AND BRINE"

Captain Newport brought 80–100 new colonists plus supplies to Jamestown in January 1608—part of the First Supply. That fall he returned with 70 more colonists including two women— the Second Supply.

13 May 1610

Dearest Mother:

I scarcely can write. Our third anniversary, and fatigue and hunger choke us all. We are lucky to have a cup of hot water each day. Last year, Captain Smith forced the savages to share their food with us after last summer's drought—now they strike at us in anger whenever we leave the fort. Few of us are strong enough to stand guard against them.

Sickness killed many of last August's new arrivals. 'Tis called "the seasoning" and is a cruel death. There is terrible head pain, fever, swelling, and worse. Some say the illness is dysentery. Most blame the river water—which tastes of slime at low tide and brine when the ocean floods in. Betwixt the savages' arrows, hunger, and sickness, the 350 planters alive when winter came are now barely 90.

'Tis painful to think the colony is failing. I survived the voyage, attacks by the savages, months of smothering heat, monstrous clouds of mosquitoes, harsh winters, and sickness. The dying moan all around me, but yet I want to stay. Virginia is a hard taskmaster but rich and beautiful, too.

I pray someone in our village will read this to you—so you will know I think of you. I hope my next letter will bring happier tidings.

Your son,
Nathaniel

By Leigh Anderson, illustrated by Craig Spearing, *Appleseeds*, © by Carus Publishing Company. Reproduced with permission. May be reproduced for classroom use. *Toolkit Texts: Short Nonfiction for American History, Colonial Times* by Stephanie Harvey and Anne Goudvis, ©2014 (Portsmouth, NH: Heinemann).

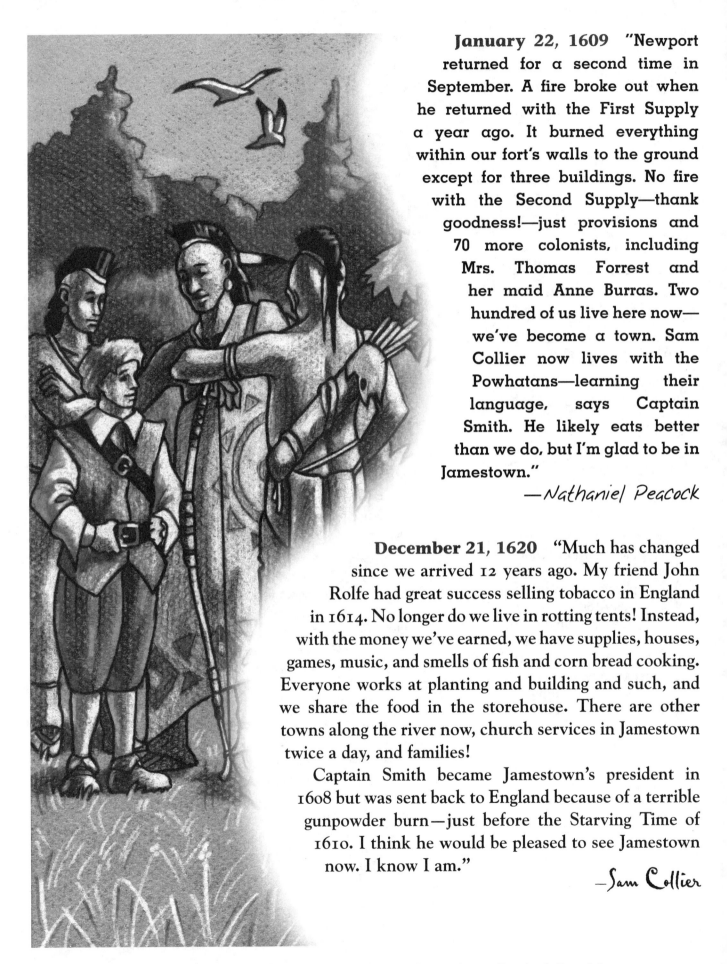

January 22, 1609 "Newport returned for a second time in September. A fire broke out when he returned with the First Supply a year ago. It burned everything within our fort's walls to the ground except for three buildings. No fire with the Second Supply—thank goodness!—just provisions and 70 more colonists, including Mrs. Thomas Forrest and her maid Anne Burras. Two hundred of us live here now—we've become a town. Sam Collier now lives with the Powhatans—learning their language, says Captain Smith. He likely eats better than we do, but I'm glad to be in Jamestown."

—Nathaniel Peacock

December 21, 1620 "Much has changed since we arrived 12 years ago. My friend John Rolfe had great success selling tobacco in England in 1614. No longer do we live in rotting tents! Instead, with the money we've earned, we have supplies, houses, games, music, and smells of fish and corn bread cooking. Everyone works at planting and building and such, and we share the food in the storehouse. There are other towns along the river now, church services in Jamestown twice a day, and families!

Captain Smith became Jamestown's president in 1608 but was sent back to England because of a terrible gunpowder burn—just before the Starving Time of 1610. I think he would be pleased to see Jamestown now. I know I am."

—Sam Collier

Plimoth Plantation

Native Peoples of the Northeast

The Northeast is often defined as the area stretching from the Great Lakes region east to the Atlantic coast and from southern Canada and Maine south through Pennsylvania to the Tidewater region of Virginia. It is a broad and diverse area in both landscape and climate. Seasons range from harsh winters and cool summers in the north to milder winters and hot, humid summers in the south.

Many Ways of Life

Five hundred years ago, when the first European explorers arrived, they discovered that the New World was occupied by two major language groups, the Iroquois and the Algonquians. Within these two groups, there were many different tribes, bands, and villages, each with its own language and way of life. Most native groups in the Northeast grew some food and did not depend solely on hunting and gathering. Others hunted, fished, and gathered wild plants so efficiently that they were able to maintain large, well-populated villages and did not need to farm.

All the groups had a deep respect for the land and the plant and animal life they depended on. Hunting, for example, was never done for sport. Aside from food, animals were a valuable source of clothing, shelter, and tools. Skins were used as bedding and clothing and sometimes as coverings for temporary shelters. Bones were fashioned into needles, scrapers, awls, and other tools. A wooden handle tied to a deer antler was turned into a garden rake.

Life on the Northeast Coast

Each group established their own way of life as they adapted to their homeland. The Penobscot, Passamaquoddy, Mi'kmaq, and Abenaki Native Americans of Maine and the Maritime Provinces in northern New England

An interpreter (above) representing Hobbamock, a 17th-century Wampanoag who lived closely with the Pilgrims at Plimoth Plantation, a living history museum in Plymouth, Massachusetts.

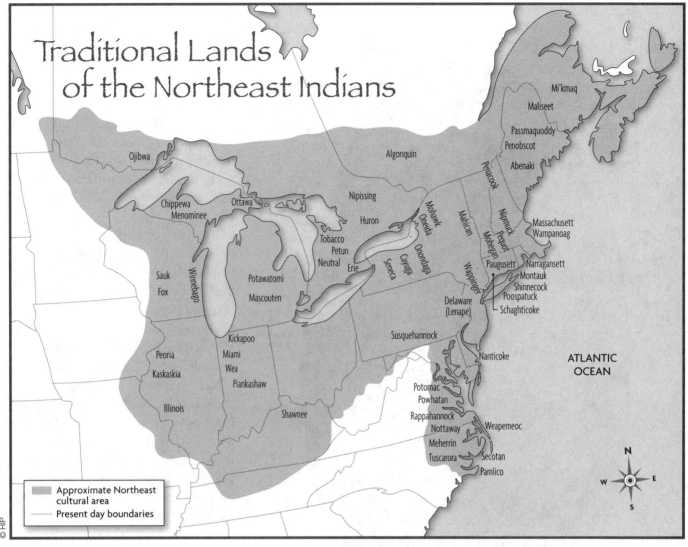

Traditional Lands of the Northeast Indians

Ojibwa
Chippewa
Menominee
Ottawa
Nipissing
Algonquin
Mi'kmaq
Maliseet
Passmaquoddy
Penobscot
Abenaki
Penacook
Nipmuck
Huron
Mohawk
Oneida
Mahican
Pequot
Mohegan
Massachusett
Wampanoag
Tobacco
Petun
Neutral
Onondaga
Cayuga
Seneca
Erie
Wappinger
Paugusett
Narragansett
Montauk
Shinnecock
Poospatuck
Schaghticoke
Sauk
Fox
Winnebago
Potawatomi
Mascouten
Delaware
(Lenape)
Kickapoo
Miami
Wea
Piankashaw
Susquehannock
Nanticoke
ATLANTIC OCEAN
Peoria
Kaskaskia
Illinois
Shawnee
Potomac
Powhatan
Rappahannock
Nottaway
Meherrin
Tuscarora
Weapemeoc
Secotan
Pamlico

Approximate Northeast cultural area
Present day boundaries

© HIP

The map above encompasses the approximate Northeast culture area.

Made of bone and wood, the tool below was probably used to hook or spear fish.

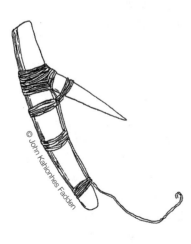

© John Kahionhes Fadden

and southeastern Canada were very different from the native peoples of southern New England. They were hunters and gatherers and organized their lives around two seasons.

In the winter, the inland forests were home to many animals for hunting, such as moose, bears, deer, and rabbits. The men trapped beavers, muskrat, and otter along the same lakes and rivers where they fished for trout, salmon, and sturgeon when it was warmer. In the Atlantic Ocean, they hunted a variety of sea mammals, such as walrus, seals, and porpoise.

In the summer, the Atlantic Ocean on one side and the St. Lawrence River on the other provided fish, clams, and oysters, which were later smoked to preserve them. Summer also was berry-picking time. The women and children gathered strawberries, blackberries, and blueberries as they ripened. With such an abundance and variety of natural resources, northern New England tribes did not need to farm. Instead, they would travel in their great canoes down the New England coast or follow the St. Lawrence River to trade with other groups for supplies they could not produce themselves.

Life in the Fertile Valleys

The homelands of the Iroquois people extended from the southern shores of Lake Ontario south through what is now western and central New York and into Pennsylvania. They called themselves the Haudenosaunee, or "People of the Longhouse." Their way of life centered on huge longhouses and large extended families. A single longhouse often held more than one hundred relatives, including grandparents, parents, children, aunts, uncles, and cousins. When a couple married, they went to live with the wife's family, and children belonged to their mother's family line, or clan. The head of the Iroquois household was a woman. Women chose the chief and had the power to remove him if he was not a good leader.

Hunting, fishing, and food gathering were considered important tasks. The Iroquois also took advantage of the fertile valleys and grew some of their food. The women were the farmers, and they were highly successful. Corn, beans, and squash were the main crops grown, with corn being the most important. Iroquois corn fields were so extensive that bushels of corn filled the longhouse granaries. They used the surplus corn to trade with people who lived in areas where the growing season was too short for corn.

© John Kahionhes Fadden

© Richard Wear/Design Pics/Corbis/HIP

The drawing of the Northeast coast campsite (above) consists of a birch-bark canoe, a wigwam, drying animal skins, and nearby access to the waterways of the Northeast.

Bears (left) and deer, important sources of food and raw materials for 17th- and 18th-century American Indians, still live in the woodlands of the Northeast today.

Plimoth Plantation

Above: Interpreters build the framework of a *neesquttow* (house with two fires) at the Wampanoag Homesite at Plimoth Plantation. The house will be covered with the pieces of bark piled to the right.

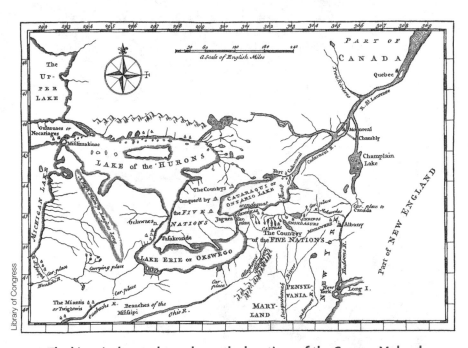

Library of Congress

The historical map above shows the locations of the Cayuga, Mohawk, Oneida, Onondaga, and Seneca nations, the original five tribes of the Iroquois Confederacy. American statesmen may have used the Iroquois Confederacy as a model when writing the U.S. Constitution.

The Iroquois also established strong trading relationships with the people along the southern New England coast, such as the Pequot and Narragansett tribes. They were especially interested in obtaining quahog (a type of clam) shells, which they fashioned into beads to make wampum belts.

Life in the Southern Regions

The native peoples of the more southerly regions lived in a variety of homelands ranging from ocean beaches to deep woodlands to rich river valleys. The Wampanoag, Narragansett, Pequot, Mohegans, and other native peoples of Southeastern New England followed the cycles of the seasons: they hunted, fished, trapped, and gathered wild plants. Like the Iroquois, they farmed their land, depending mostly on corn, beans, and squash. Men built *weetuash* (houses) out of cedar saplings covered with chestnut or elm bark. People traveled in dug-out canoes called *mishoonash*, made from logs of white pine or cedar. A mishoon could fit up to 40 people. The women cared for the homes and gardens, but unlike the Iroquois, they did not select the leaders. However, women often became chiefs, particularly in southern New England.

There are an estimated 157,000 native people living in the Northeast of the United States today. Penobscots, Mi'kmaq, Pequots, Wampanoags, Abenakis, Narragansetts, Mohawks, Mohegans, and others live in cities, towns, and rural areas, as well as on reservation lands set aside for their ancestors long ago. They are doctors, lawyers, teachers, construction workers, farmers, artists, and even Native American chiefs. They live much like their non–Native American neighbors. They are proud of their rich history and strive to pass on their culture and heritage to future generations.

American Indian Population of the Northeast

Connecticut	31,140
Delaware	9,899
District of Columbia	6,521
Maine	18,482
Maryland	58,657
Massachusetts	50,705
New Hampshire	10,524
New Jersey	70,716
New York	221,058
Pennsylvania	81,092
Rhode Island	14,394
Vermont	7,379
Virginia	80,924

These population numbers reflect any American Indian or Alaskan Native living in the Northeast at the time of the 2010 census. There is no distinction between members of original Northeast tribes still living in the area and American Indians from different culture areas (Northeast Coast or Southwest, for example) who have moved to the Northeast. These numbers do not include Northeast Indians living outside of the Northeast.

Word Lore

hickory • wigwam • caribou • squash

Although many original Northeast Native American languages are no longer spoken, they are far from gone. Modern English or French versions of native words that were recorded in the 1500s and 1600s by early missionaries and settlers still cover our maps and pepper our conversations.

These now-familiar words made their way into North American English and French for several reasons. European settlers, being unfamiliar with animals native to North America, used the Native American terms for them. Moose, muskrat, caribou, skunk, opossum, and woodchuck are some examples. Settlers also adopted native place names, giving us Canada, Ottawa, Connecticut, Massachusetts, Michigan, Wisconsin, Illinois, Ohio, Miami, and Ontario.

Other Northeast Native American words commonly used today include succotash, squash, wampum, tomahawk, hickory, hominy, manitou, sagamore, and powwow. Native words linger like natural music and continue to reach far beyond their points of origin to enrich our conversations.

wampum • tomahawk • powwow • moose • hominy

By Trudie Lamb Richmond, *Cobblestone*, © by Carus Publishing Company. Reproduced with permission.
May be reproduced for classroom use. *Toolkit Texts: Short Nonfiction for American History, Colonial Times*
by Stephanie Harvey and Anne Goudvis, ©2014 (Portsmouth, NH: Heinemann).

THE FIRST VIRGINIANS

North Wind Picture Archives

When Powhatan died, his brother Opechancanough became the supreme chief. Opechancanough led uprisings against the English settlers for taking over his people's land and pushing them onto poorer soil.

The English often called the native people "savages" because they did not live according to English customs. The English believed that their own ways of dressing and living and believing were the right ways. For the most part, they did not value the Virginia Native Americans' ways.

"We hope to plant a nation/Where none before hath stood," sang the English about Virginia. They obviously did not understand that native peoples already lived in the New World—ancient and proud nations that had established systems of government and religion, as well as art and music and firmly implanted cultures. Instead, the English believed America was inhabited by "savages."

Members of the Virginia Company did get an unpleasant welcome while looking for a settlement site: "At our landing, there came many . . . Savages to resist us with their Bowes and Arrowes, in a most warlike manner. . . ." But the Native Americans also helped the English. Settler George Percy acknowledged that "[i]t pleased God, after a while to send . . . our mortall enemies [the Indians] to releeve us . . . Bread, Corne, Fish, and Flesh . . . otherwise we had perished."

In 1607, there were perhaps 14,000 to 20,000 native people living near the Chesapeake Bay in Virginia. Most were Algonquian, Siouan, and Iroquoian speakers. The Algonquian-speaking Powhatan chiefdom, located around the southern part of the bay, was led by the supreme chief, Powhatan. Comprising about 30 or so tribes, these people lived in small villages, each ruled by a *werowance*, or chief. Surrounded by fields, their houses were like **arbors** in that they were built from small trees that were bent over, tied, and then covered with woven mats.

Using bows and arrows, spears, clubs, snares, and traps, the native men hunted deer, bear, turkey, and smaller game for both food and **pelts**. Sailing the bay and its rivers in wooden dugout canoes, they employed bone hooks, nets, spears, bows and arrows, and **weirs** to catch a variety of fish. And the men practiced for war: They painted themselves until they were "monstrous to behould," as Captain John Smith observed.

Most of the work around the villages was left to the native women. Along with the children, women grew corn, squash, beans, and other crops. They gathered fruits, herbs, nuts, and roots, and cooked, sewed, wove, and made pottery.

Although Smith referred to them as "savages," he also admired the Native Americans. They understood the natural world and knew "the places most frequented with Deare, Beasts, Fish, Foule, Rootes, and Berries." They were "generally tall and straight . . . [and able] to lie in the woods under a tree by a fire in the worst of winter." They were good parents and "doe love children verie dearly," and some villages even had a temple and priests.

The growth of tobacco as a primary crop—and the land it required—brought more conflict with the native people after 1610. There was sporadic violence and a brief period of peace between the two groups until 1622. Powhatan had died in 1618, and his brother Opechancanough had become the leader. Opechancanough saw

These samples of Native American arrow points have been found in excavations at Jamestown.

Preservation Virginia

how the English plantations had pushed his people onto poorer land. In March 1622, his warriors attacked and killed one-third of the settlers. This uprising started a war that lasted nearly 10 years. In 1644, with the native peoples still being pushed from their land, Opechancanough organized another rebellion. By then, however, they were outnumbered and outgunned, and were crushed easily.

The Powhatans would be just one of many Native American groups to see their way of life disrupted and altered by the arrival of colonists in North America.

Arbors *are shady resting places often made of a framework on which climbing shrubs are grown.*

Pelts *are animal skins that still have fur on them.*

Weirs *are basket-like traps placed in streams to catch fish.*

FAST FACT

TWO STATE-RECOGNIZED INDIAN RESERVATIONS REMAIN IN EXISTENCE TODAY IN VIRGINIA. THEY ARE THE MATTAPONI AND THE PAMUNKEY, LOCATED NEAR WEST POINT.

© James P. Rowan

A Native American dwelling (or "yehakin" in Algonquian) was built by bending saplings and covering them with woven mats, as shown in this replica at Jamestown Settlement.

Africans in Colonial America

The Portuguese pioneered the transatlantic slave trade in the mid-1500s.

They bought captives on the West African coast from African merchants and from African rulers and their agents. The Portuguese then transported these captives to work in their colony of Brazil in South America, and, after signing agreements with Spain, to the Spanish colonies in the Americas. Some of these Africans had already been enslaved in Africa as the result of wars between African states or civil wars between African rulers. Others had been captured by bandits and outlaws and sold illegally to Portuguese merchants. In a few cases, African courts had condemned them to slavery for crimes they, or sometimes members of their families, had committed.

A Practice Grows

Neither English nor Dutch merchants bought slaves in Africa in the 1500s. Merchants of both nations did visit and trade with African states from the 1550s onward, but purchased only gold, cloth, ivory, and other African products. In one or two rare cases, they captured Africans when they raided the coast. For the most part, they obtained slaves by attacking Portuguese ships that were carrying the Africans to Spanish America. They then resold the captured Africans to the English and Dutch colonies in South America, the Caribbean, and North America. Only in the late

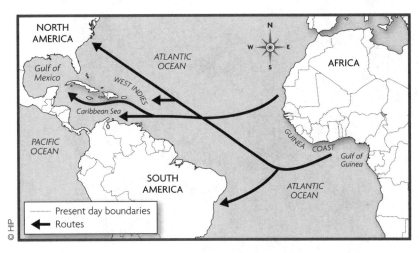

The Atlantic slave trade consisted of more than 35,000 slave voyages that forcibly transported over 12 million Africans to the Americas between the sixteenth and nineteenth centuries.

By John K. Thornton, *Footprints*, © by Carus Publishing Company. Reproduced with permission.
May be reproduced for classroom use. *Toolkit Texts: Short Nonfiction for American History, Colonial Times*
by Stephanie Harvey and Anne Goudvis, ©2014 (Portsmouth, NH: Heinemann).

North Wind Picture Archives

Library of Congress

Top: Slaves unload rice barges in South Carolina.

Bottom: Under the watchful eye of an overseer, slaves work at a sugar mill in the Caribbean in the 1600s.

1630s did the Dutch and English begin buying slaves in Africa for their colonies in America. To do so, they used the same techniques as the Portuguese.

Initially, the English slave trade was directed to Barbados in the Caribbean; the Dutch trade, to Brazil and then to colonies in South America. The first slaves to be brought directly from Africa to North America came to New Amsterdam (present-day New York City) in 1653. Many of these slaves were promptly sold to the English colonists to work on plantations in the Chesapeake Bay area (present-day Virginia, Maryland, and Delaware). The direct slave trade to North America was slow to develop. At first, only Dutch ships brought slaves. However, after the English took control of the Dutch colony of New York in 1664, most new slaves came from the Caribbean islands rather than from Africa. English merchants started buying slaves again from Africa after 1700.

Slavery Laws Evolve

At first, the English and Dutch did not have a code of laws for slaveowners. They held some slaves for life, others they released after a period of years. Many of the first Africans in America came from Angola on the west-central coast of Africa, and some of them were Christians.

Toward the end of the 1660s, the number of enslaved people brought to America greatly increased. They came mostly from West Africa and were less likely to be Christian. Ideas about slavery began to change, and the belief that the condition of slavery was life-long and **inheritable** gradually became

Inheritable, in this context, means one was born a slave if one or both parents were slaves.

The Colonial Williamsburg Foundation

Top: To the delight of his family, a child dances to the music of a fiddler (at far right) in the slave quarters of the Knickerbocker Mansion in New York, in the 1700s.

Middle: A tobacco ship in the Virginia Colony's James River prepares to take on cargo.

Bottom: Black carpenters maneuver a boat into position to complete construction.

fixed in law after 1660. By the 1720s, it had also become law that children born of free mothers by slave fathers had to remain slaves.

Communities Are Established

The early slaves in the Chesapeake Bay area worked largely in tobacco fields and were often housed together or mixed with indentured servants from Europe. In Dutch New Amsterdam, however, many lived in a small village and worked in municipal (city) construction as well as agriculture. After 1670, African slaves and their descendants throughout the Americas tended to be housed separately from other servants or workers. They lived in "quarters" that resembled villages, consisting of a few houses, where they developed their own distinctive lifestyle. Only those slaves who performed personal service or lived in towns and cities (mostly in the Northern colonies) might live intermixed with other servants of different origins.

Life for many Africans working in America was hard, and, for the earliest to arrive, it was also short. The high death rate made it difficult for families and communities to form. But by the 1730s, the descendants of the earliest slaves were living longer, and families began to form. Soon, African American slaves were having enough children to keep their population stable, and, as a result, the importation of Africans declined.

The Chesapeake Bay region more or less stopped importing slaves from Africa in the 1770s, as did most of the urban areas in the North. Newer colonies, such as South Carolina, which began large-scale importation of Africans only in the 1720s, and French Louisiana, continued to import Africans, as the plantation economy expanded to rely on slave labor.

Check out these reconstructed 1700s slave cabins at Carter's Grove near Williamsburg, Virginia. Can you find the fireplace in the reconstructed cabin above?

African Influences in a New Land

Enslaved Africans arriving in North America during the period of the slave trade brought skills, cultural practices, and beliefs from their homeland. Many already knew how to cultivate tobacco and rice, two of the more important cash crops in Colonial America. Some were Christians, and some Muslims. Many, however, came from other religious traditions and held other religious ideas, such as the belief that their dead ancestors played a role in shaping their lives.

Other religious and medical practices from Africa shaped cultural life during these times.

Two of the strongest cultural influences of Africa in America were music and dance. Rhythmic African musical styles, as well as a few musical instruments (notably the banjo), were imported from Africa, and soon African Americans were mixing local and African musical traditions. The styles they created became one of the hallmarks of American culture.

ANGELO'S STORY

Scholarship means knowledge resulting from study and research in a particular field.

Wattle and mud daub is an interweaving of rods and twigs overlaid with clay and used as a building material.

A hierarchy is a categorization of people according to ability or status.

FAST FACT

THE PORTUGUESE GAVE THE NAME "ANGOLA" TO NDONGO. THE ANGOLANS PLAYED A VARIETY OF MUSICAL INSTRUMENTS, INCLUDING DRUMS, TAMBOURINES, FLUTES, BELLS, HORNS, AND LUTES.

Until recently, not much was known about the first Africans to come to Virginia. They certainly came unwillingly, part of a group captured by the Portuguese army from the West Central African land of Ndongo in 1619.

While on their way to the Spanish colony of Mexico as slaves, their ship was seized by English privateers. Some of those Africans on board then were brought to Virginia and sold as servants or slaves to tobacco planters.

But recent scholarship has revealed more detailed information about the origins of these first Africans to the New World, including one in particular—a woman named Angelo.

In Ndongo, Angelo's people lived either in small palisaded villages of several hundred people or in large towns with thousands of inhabitants. Houses, built of wattle and mud daub, were round or rectangular and roofed with palm leaves. They had only one room, low doors, and a central hearth that provided both light and heat.

Angelo's diet included bread made from pounded millet grain, as well as yams, beans, and peas. The women grew those crops, as well as tobacco. The men raised goats, cattle, and sheep, and hunted and fished for food.

In addition to farming, many of Angelo's people were craftsmen who made tools and weapons of fine steel. They also melted and worked copper, lead, silver, and other metals into jewelry and other items. The Ndongo people used nzimbu shells and copper bracelets called mantillas as money at the local markets.

Cloth was made by pounding the bark from certain trees to produce thin threads for weaving. Most people of Ndongo wore simple garments made of woven bark cloth that tied around the waist and fell to the knees. Men of higher status wore netted vests and capes. Some wore animal skins around their waists and sandals or boots on their feet.

In Ndongo, local authorities called sobas had great influence and governed alongside powerful family leaders. Ndongo society had a definite hierarchy that ranged from political and military elites and religious leaders at the top, down to commoners and servants or slaves. Those considered superior in status wore more elaborate clothing, had better houses, and carried symbols of authority such as staffs. Their religion combined traditional Ndongo beliefs with Christian concepts that had been introduced by the Portuguese. People built large shrines to worship local gods, and craftsmen carved elaborate religious objects out of wood.

Before she was taken from Ndongo, Angelo received religious instruction in the Catholic faith. She took the Christian name "Angela" at her baptism, but the name was recorded incorrectly as "Angelo" by the English after her arrival in Virginia. By 1625, Angelo belonged to a prominent Virginia planter named William Peirce, who also held several English indentured servants. It is not known whether Angelo ever regained her freedom.

North Wind Picture Archives

© Dynamic Graphics/Jupiterimages/Getty Images/HIP

"Why should you destroy us, who have provided you with food?"

POWHATAN, WAHUNSONACOCK (POWHATAN), C. 1609
SPEAKING TO JOHN SMITH

I am now grown old, and must soon die; and the succession must descend, in order, to my brothers, Poitchapan, Openkankanough, and Catataugh, and then to my sisters, and their two daughters. I wish their experience was equal to mine and that your love to us might not be less than ours to you. Why should you take by force that from us which you can have by love? Why should you destroy us, who have provided you with food? What can you get by war? We can hide our provisions, and fly into the woods; and then you must consequently famish by wronging your friends. What is the cause of your jealousy? You see us unarmed, and willing to supply your wants, if you will come in a friendly manner, and not with swords and guns, as to invade an enemy.

I am not so simple, as not to know it is better to eat good meat, lie well, and sleep quietly with my women and children; to laugh and be merry with the English; and, being their friend, to have copper, hatchets, and whatever else I want, than to fly from all to lie cold in the woods, feed upon acorns, roots, and such trash, and to be son hunted, that I cannot rest, eat, or sleep. . . . I, therefore, exhort you to peaceable councils; and, above all, I insist that the guns and swords, the cause of all our jealousy and uneasiness, be removed and sent away.

Elections in the Colonies

The colonists who came to America believed in popular sovereignty—rule by the people. They wanted a system that was different from the British system, in which members of Parliament came from the gentry (upper class) and were expected to represent everyone fairly, including the overseas colonies. In 1619, for example, members of the Virginia House of Burgesses had to live and own property in the district they represented, which in theory meant that they could be more responsive to the needs of the voters.

Election Laws

The colonists did not give everyone the right to vote. Politics was considered a male activity. At first, only men who owned property could vote. The colonists thought that one reason to have government was to protect property; therefore, those who controlled government were owners of property. Since men without property did not pay much in taxes, people generally believed that they should not be allowed to decide what the taxes would be. But since land in the colonies was both more plentiful and cheaper than it was in England or Europe, many

American colonists were willing to make the "ultimate sacrifice" for the right to govern themselves. The engraving above shows American patriot Nathan Hale—convicted, without a trial, for spying—before he was hanged by the British in 1776.

more men were property owners and could participate in voting for those who governed them.

Some colonies had rules requiring that a person live in the colony for a certain amount of time before he could vote. These laws were meant to ensure that voters cared about the colony. Other requirements to vote concerned race, religion, and gender. African Americans, even if they were free, could not vote. Some men kept women from voting by saying that voting would overtax the female intelligence!

VOTES FOR WOMEN,

For the work of a day,
For the taxes we pay,
For the Laws we obey,
We want something to say.

6342

When John Adams went to participate in the First Continental Congress in 1774, his wife, Abigail (above), begged him to "remember the ladies" when making decisions about the future of the American colonies.

A postcard (left) sums up the feelings of women in the 20th century in one sentiment: the demand for a role in elections.

By Carolyn Gard, Cobblestone, © by Carus Publishing Company. Reproduced with permission.
May be reproduced for classroom use. Toolkit Texts: Short Nonfiction for American History, Colonial Times by Stephanie Harvey and Anne Goudvis, ©2014 (Portsmouth, NH: Heinemann).

British Control

Since the British government appointed the governors and members of the upper house of the colonial legislatures, the colonists voted only for members of the lower house of the legislatures and local officials. Voters did not get much information about the candidates, and they often voted only to remove an officeholder who had misbehaved.

Most colonies had no specific nominating procedure. Men went to the polls and voted for anyone they pleased. Sometimes a group of people with similar interests would get together and persuade someone who thought as the group did to run for office.

The most important part of campaigning was personal contact. Candidates tried to meet as many people as they could and to shake as many hands as possible. They went to militia training sessions, court proceedings, and church meetings.

Colonial elections were held whenever an important issue came up or when the governor dismissed the assembly and new delegates had to be chosen. People learned about the elections through notices, called broadsides, that were read in churches or posted in towns. Later, newspapers carried election notices. Sometimes, to help a particular candidate win, election dates were not announced in certain areas.

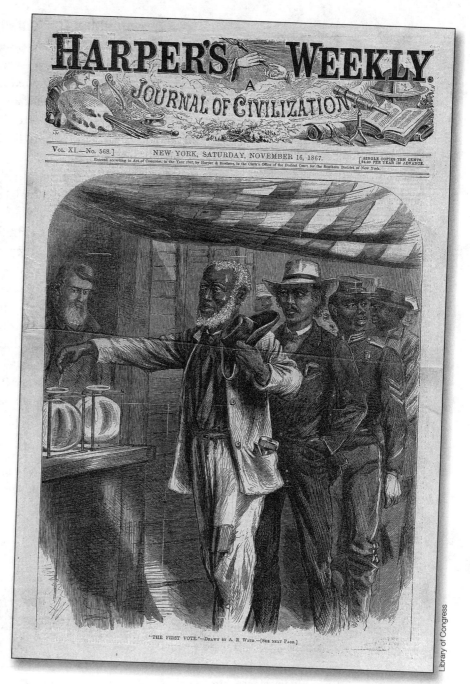

This engraving shows an African American artisan voting for the first time in 1867 by dropping his "ballot" in one of two bowls.

Election Day

On Election Day, voters came from all over the district to the polling place. Each voter approached the table, stated his name, and announced his vote. Many people thought that this method was more honest than a secret paper ballot.

About fifty to eighty percent of the white males in the colonies could vote, but only ten to forty percent of them normally cast their ballots in an election. One reason for the low turnout was the long distances over rough roads that voters had to travel. To vote, men would have to be gone from home for a day or two, and farmers could not afford to leave their crops for that long.

THE ILLUSTRATED LONDON NEWS

No. 1950—VOL. LXIX.   SATURDAY, DECEMBER 9, 1876.   WITH TWO SUPPLEMENTS [SIXPENCE

THE PRESIDENTIAL ELECTION IN AMERICA: FRAUDULENT VOTERS IN CUSTODY AT THE UNITED STATES CIRCUIT COURT, NEW YORK.

Library of Congress

Colonial Discontent

As the British increased restrictions, colonists rebelled and wanted to have a voice in how they were governed. In 1749, one writer described the right to vote this way: "'Tis a glorious privilege! and methinks every one of you should be fond of all Opportunities to put in your claim to it, and shew [show] what a Right you enjoy beyond some others of your Fellow Subjects."

As the American Revolution neared, politics grew more intense. The colonial delegates to the assemblies took control of local issues, and the British-appointed governors had to bargain with them. To get more people to vote, colonies eased their requirements to own property, nominations became more open, the number of polling places increased, and voters used secret ballots.

The framers of the Constitution knew that freedoms are preserved by voting. They included the right to vote (suffrage) in the document, which has since been amended several times to extend suffrage to nonwhite, nonmale citizens, such as African American men and all women, as well as to younger and less-well-off citizens.

Fraudulent (cheating) voters were a problem during and after the colonial period. This 1876 *London News* sketch shows people who had broken the voting law being put in jail.

GROUP	VOTING RIGHTS
Wealthy, upper-class white men	Could vote and hold public office
Middle-class white men	Could vote, but few held public office
Lower-class white men	Could not vote and most were illiterate
Women	Could not vote
Indentured servants (mostly white)	Could not vote
Slaves	Could not vote

The basic principle that governed voting in Colonial America was that voters should have a "stake in society." Leaders believed that the vote should be restricted to men who owned property and paid taxes.

By Carolyn Gard, *Cobblestone*, © by Carus Publishing Company. Reproduced with permission. May be reproduced for classroom use. *Toolkit Texts: Short Nonfiction for American History, Colonial Times* by Stephanie Harvey and Anne Goudvis, ©2014 (Portsmouth, NH: Heinemann).

North Wind Picture Archives

RELIGIOUS FREEDOM
IN COLONIAL AMERICA

A wood engraving of New England Puritans walking to church in the snow.

America's first colonists came to the New World in search of religious freedom. Yet all the early colonies—whether settled by the French, Spanish, Dutch, or English—set up established or state-supported churches patterned after the government-run churches of Europe. Many of the first settlers came from countries where church and government had long been connected, and they had not been free to choose a religion.

Things did not seem much different for them in America at first. The original colonial governments required all residents to support a specific church, regardless of individual religious beliefs. In Virginia (the first permanent English settlement in

America), for example, all households were taxed to support the Anglican Church—just as in England. Several other southern colonies also named the Anglican Church as their state church.

RELIGIOUS FREEDOM FOR SOME

Most of the New England colonists, however, did not want to re-create England's official church in their new homeland. These were the Puritans. They accused the Anglicans of putting too much stress on ritual aspects and not enough on Biblical teachings. In the New World, the Puritans hoped to worship without Anglican interference. Yet, although they sought religious freedom for themselves in America,

Picture Collection, The New York Public Library, Astor, Lenox and Tilden Foundations

Government officials threatened to arrest Roger Williams and ship him back to England because he refused to stop discussions of freedom of religion. Williams fled three days before a blizzard and walked through deep snow for 105 miles to Rhode Island.

Dissent is a difference of opinion, or a disagreement.

Banished means forced by official orders to leave a place.

A **haven** is a safe place.

Repealed means recalled, or reversed.

Persecution is the act of being harassed or punished for one's beliefs, race, or religion.

they did not extend that freedom to others. Consequently, every New Englander was compelled by law to support and attend the local Puritan (also called Congregational) church. Any religious **dissent** was prohibited. Catholics and non-Puritan Protestants, such as Quakers, sometimes were fined, imprisoned, whipped, or **banished** by government officials. Those rejecting Puritanism, warned one Puritan leader, "shall have free liberty to keep away from us, and . . . be gone as fast as they can."

RELIGIOUS FREEDOM FOR ALL

Not every American colony refused to allow religious freedom. More than a century before the Bill of Rights was written, three colonies were founded on precisely the issue of guaranteeing religious choice.

Maryland, established by the Calvert family in 1634, was a **haven** for England's much-persecuted Catholics. Maryland's founders offered religious freedom to all Christian settlers, Protestant or Catholic. These rights were confirmed in 1649 by the Act of Toleration, considered a milestone of religious liberty. Unfortunately, the act proved to be short-lived. When Anglicans outnumbered Catholics in Maryland in the late 1600s, the colony's new Anglican leaders **repealed** the act. The Anglican Church became the state church of Maryland.

In 1635, Massachusetts's Puritan rulers banished a minister named Roger Williams for daring to criticize the colony's close bond between

church and government. Soon after, Williams founded Rhode Island, the first American colony to guarantee separation of church and state. He unconditionally supported religious liberty for all. No Rhode Islander, the colonial charter promised, would be "punished, disquieted, or called in question for any differences in opinion on matters of religion." The colony quickly attracted Catholics, Jews, Baptists, and others fleeing **persecution** elsewhere in America and in Europe.

About fifty years later, Englishman William Penn founded the colony of Pennsylvania as a refuge for his fellow Quakers. Quakers had been persecuted violently in both England and America. They emphasized pacifism (peacefulness) and the equality of all people before God. Established in 1681 by Penn, the colony offered religious freedom to all its residents, Christian and non-Christian. Penn's "holy experiment," as he called it, in religious freedom was a great success. One of the wealthiest American colonies by the start of the Revolutionary War, Pennsylvania also was one of the most heavily populated. During the 1700s, people from all over Europe flocked to the colony in the hope of enjoying the religious liberty guaranteed in its constitution. Pennsylvania became home to more than four hundred different religious groups—the most religiously diverse colony in the New World.

By showing that people of many religions could live together peacefully, Pennsylvania and Rhode Island helped promote an acceptance of religious diversity among Americans. And along with this tolerance came an important change in the colonial population.

John Winthrop served as governor of Massachusetts and was one of the most famous Puritan leaders. He was governor when both Roger Williams and Anne Hutchinson were banned from the colony for their religious beliefs.

North Wind Picture Archives

FREEDOM ATTRACTS NEWCOMERS

From about 1700 on, America's population began to become more diverse. People from many different countries and faiths flocked to the New World. When the Revolutionary War began in 1775, nine of the original thirteen colonies still had state-run churches: the Anglican Church in Virginia, Maryland, North Carolina, South Carolina, Georgia, and New York and the Congregational Church in Massachusetts, Connecticut, and New Hampshire. But in almost all these colonies, dissenters now outnumbered members of established churches! No one religious group remained large enough to control every other group.

Even the once-powerful Massachusetts Puritans were forced to make important **concessions** to dissenters. They began to permit Baptists and other non-Puritans to use income from taxes to support their own churches. Local governments throughout the colonies were finding it increasingly difficult to enforce belief in one religion.

Thus, the pattern of religious persecution slowly was being replaced by religious freedom. The way was paved for the Bill of Rights, with its guarantee of full religious liberty for all Americans.

Concessions are acknowledgments that certain points are true or just.

Puritan Psalm Book

Library of Congress/HIP

COLONY	OFFICIAL RELIGION(S)
Virginia	Anglican
Massachusetts	Puritan/Congregational
Rhode Island	Religious freedom: Catholics, Jews, Baptists, Quakers and others all welcomed
Pennsylvania	Quakers, other religions welcomed
New Hampshire	Puritan/Congregational
New York	Anglican but allowed other religions
Maryland	Anglican, Catholic until 1692
Connecticut	Puritan/Congregational
Delaware	Anglican but allowed other religions
North Carolina	Anglican but allowed other religions
New Jersey	Anglican but allowed other religions
South Carolina	Anglican but allowed other religions
Georgia	Anglican

QUAKERS

The Society of Friends, also called The Quakers, were a religious group that worshipped in ways totally different from other religions in Colonial America. They did not have paid ministers or priests, and they did not use any of the sacraments that other religions did, such as baptism and communion. They did not follow the Bible or the teachings of Jesus as closely as other religions. They believed in "the inner light." In a Quaker church service, the members sat in silence until one of them felt inspired to speak. Because they were persecuted in other countries, many Quakers came to America looking for religious freedom. They believed in peace, justice, and equality for everyone, including Native Americans. They would also become the first supporters of abolitionism, speaking out against slavery. However, because of their beliefs, Quakers were also persecuted and sometimes even executed in Colonial America.

By Louise Chipley Slavicek, *Cobblestone*, © by Carus Publishing Company. Reproduced with permission.
May be reproduced for classroom use. *Toolkit Texts: Short Nonfiction for American History, Colonial Times*
by Stephanie Harvey and Anne Goudvis, ©2014 (Portsmouth, NH: Heinemann).

What to Wear?

Three hundred years ago, children's clothing looked very different from the way it looks today. When we look at the clothes many children wore, they look quite fancy and uncomfortable. In fact, just like today, children wore clothes very much like their parents' clothes.

In the 1700s, all clothing was made of natural fabrics such as wool, linen, and sometimes cotton. In wealthy families, children wore fabric woven to be soft and fine. In poor families, children wore fabric that was much rougher. There were no stores where you could buy these clothes, though. Usually, children's clothing was made by their mothers. In wealthy families, seamstresses and tailors made clothes.

All little children wore the same kinds of clothes. These were called frocks. To us, these frocks look like long dresses. But even little boys wore these until they were "breeched" (this means old enough to wear breeches, or pants). This happened when a boy was about 4 years old.

Let's look at some of the other clothes that colonial children wore.

Mrs. Freake and Baby Mary,
by an unidentified artist.

By Meg Galante-DeAngelis, *Appleseeds*, © by Carus Publishing Company. Reproduced with permission. May be reproduced for classroom use. *Toolkit Texts: Short Nonfiction for American History, Colonial Times* by Stephanie Harvey and Anne Goudvis, ©2014 (Portsmouth, NH: Heinemann).

Underwear

Girls wore several petticoats at the same time.

Pockets were worn on top of the petticoat and under the skirt of the dress.

David Meade, Jr., by Thomas Hudson.

Shirts were considered underwear, always covered with a jacket or a vest.

Stays, undergarments used to support the ribcage, were worn by boys and girls to promote good posture. Toddlers wore soft stays, but older children wore stays made of bone. Boys wore stays until they were between 4 and 7 years old. Girls wore stays their entire lives.

Hats

All children, rich or poor, wore hats. They even wore caps to bed.

Girls wore caps inside and outside.

Outside, girls often wore skimmers over their caps. Long ribbons tied around the back of the head kept the skimmer on.

Babies wore soft Pudding Caps to protect their head in case they fell.

Outerwear

All boys and girls wore frocks (long dresses) when they were small. As girls got older, they continued to wear frocks just like their mothers did. Boys wore long frock coats and breeches, pants that end just below the knee.

David, Joanna, and Abigail Mason,
by an unidentified artist.

Skeleton suits were worn by little boys. The shirt buttoned into the waist of the pants. They were tight-fitting and high-waisted.

Sometimes toddlers' frocks had strips of fabric sewn to the shoulder. Parents used these to prevent the child from falling. Older girls' frocks had similar strips of fabric, known as "hanging sleeves." They were a symbol that the girl still needed guidance from her parents.

Girls wore hats all the time, even in the house.

A calash was a fancy bonnet that looked like a covered wagon.	Slave girls often wore a scarf tied on their head.	Sometimes boys wore knit hats. Sometimes the maker would knit words of freedom on the hat. These special caps were called Liberty Caps.

By Meg Galante-DeAngelis, *Appleseeds*, © by Carus Publishing Company. Reproduced with permission. May be reproduced for classroom use. *Toolkit Texts: Short Nonfiction for American History, Colonial Times* by Stephanie Harvey and Anne Goudvis, ©2014 (Portsmouth, NH: Heinemann).

Craftsmen, Artisans, & Tradesmen

THERE WAS NOT MUCH ROOM on the first ships to America. Early settlers brought with them only a small amount of furniture, clothes, tools, kitchenware, and other goods for their new homes. When they arrived in the New World, they found no shops or factories to provide them with goods, so they had to make whatever else they needed themselves or wait for another ship from England to arrive with more supplies.

A lot of colonists did depend on England for fabric and clothing, furniture, iron tools, and other supplies. Since most of the colonies were settled to provide the mother country with raw materials, these colonists could trade their raw materials, such

Winterthur Museum

A room at Winterthur Museum contains the woodworking shop of the Dominy family of East Hampton, New York. Beginning in the mid-1700s, three generations of family members made furniture, clock cases, and mill parts in the carpenter's shop and clock gears and movements in a clock shop alongside their home. Both shops were re-created with their original equipment.

as pine tar, turpentine, tobacco, and wood, for goods made in England. But not all colonists had products to sell to England or could afford imported goods, so many made what they needed themselves. The men cut down trees and used lumber from them to build their homes and furniture. The women made soap and candles and grew flax and raised sheep to provide linen and wool thread to weave into cloth.

BLACKSMITH

Skills for a New World

Many of the earliest settlers were skilled craftsmen when they arrived. The first blacksmith in America was James Reed, who arrived in Jamestown in 1607. Blacksmiths were among the most important craftsmen because they could repair the tools, chains, and other imported iron products colonists depended on. They also made fireplace andirons and sometimes forged new ax blades to cut wood, chains to haul lumber, and even nails to build houses. Women relied on the blacksmith to mend and make pot handles, forks, ladles, hooks, and cooking spits.

John Alden came to Plymouth in 1630 on the Mayflower. He was a cooper, someone who made tubs, pails, and barrels. Benjamin Franklin's father, Josiah, who came to this country in 1638, was a dyer (someone who colored newly woven cloth) but found little demand for his trade. He became a tallow chandler (candle maker) and soap boiler instead. At age ten, Ben worked in his father's Boston shop, cutting wicks for the candles and filling the molds.

Many goods were imported from England. The British government even imposed laws that made it difficult for colonial craftsmen to produce things that English merchants wished to sell to them. But the growing need for material goods encouraged more and more people to try their hands at various crafts in the New World. Men who might never have dared to open shops as masters in England became chandlers, tailors, shoemakers, and such in the colonies.

Self Taught and Homemade

To supplement the limited imported goods available, the settlers made many necessities in the home. Self-taught woodworkers made farm and household items from wood, the most abundant raw material. Among these items were plows,

COOPER

SHOEMAKER

BRICK MAKER

COACH MAKER

bowls, kitchen utensils, and furniture. Over the years, cabinetmaking became one of the most successful early American crafts.

Women and children in most rural households used the spinning wheel to make woolen thread from the fleece of family sheep and linen thread from homegrown flax. Men wove the thread into clothing, bedding, and table linens. In Virginia, a traveling weaver sometimes spent months at a planter's home weaving cloth for the family.

As settlements began to prosper, colonists were able to pay to have things made for them, and persons skilled in a craft found they could make a living from their trade, although many had to work at more than one trade to make ends meet. Carpenters in rural areas also served as cabinet-makers, wagon makers, and coffin makers. The early craftsman working out of his home and, later, a nearby shop often needed a sideline or two if business was not steady enough.

The nature of some trades required craftsmen to go where the work was. An itinerant cobbler carried his tools, leather, and small workbench on his back, repairing footwear in people's homes. Tinkers, handymen who traveled with kits called "pigs," repaired small household items and carried molds to produce, among other things, pewter buttons and spoons. Traveling candle makers sometimes went from house to house with their molds, offering their services to families who had stored up grease to be made into candles.

From Simple to Elaborate

Before very long, goods that had once been luxuries became staples, and the number and variety of craftsmen grew. The products they made often differed from colony to colony. A silversmith in a large city was more likely to make large, elaborate items that the city's wealthy population could buy, while his fellow craftsman in the country might have spent more time making small items, repairing larger ones, and importing a few more elaborate

By Robert D. San Souci, *Cobblestone*, © by Carus Publishing Company. Reproduced with permission. Woodcuts from *1800 Woodcuts by Thomas Bewick and His School*, Dover Publications, Inc., 1962. May be reproduced for classroom use. *Toolkit Texts: Short Nonfiction for American History, Colonial Times* by Stephanie Harvey and Anne Goudvis, ©2014 (Portsmouth, NH: Heinemann).

pieces for those who wanted them. Cabinetmakers in Philadelphia produced fancy decorated furniture, but those in Virginia found that their customers preferred well-built, less ornamented pieces. Although there were many similarities in the work of craftsmen around the colonies, there also were differences in style and methods of work because of the colonists' different backgrounds.

POTTER

The best craftsmen gathered in well-to-do coastal cities such as New York and Philadelphia where the large population could support them. By 1647, Boston boasted professional weavers, leather workers, felt makers, furriers, rope makers, and brick and tile makers. Further growth drew even more craftspeople to the colonies. A shipload of Irish immigrants arriving at Boston in 1716 included, among the men, an anchor and ship smith, house carpenter, ship joiner (carpenter), carver, cooper, shoemaker, currier (leather tanner), tailor, book printer, nailer, and locksmith. The women included a milliner (hat maker), ribbon weaver, lace weaver, button maker, and potter.

Metalworkers included coppersmiths, silversmiths, goldsmiths, and tinsmiths who had learned their trades in Europe. Many worked with several metals. Braziers (who worked with brass) produced pots, pans, door knockers, and other items. Plumbers worked with lead, often rolling or casting it into pipes.

Workers in wood were vital to the colonies. They built homes, furniture, tools, and household wooden ware. Early settlers had made their own tools, wooden ware, and furniture, as well as their homes and barns. As craftsmen specialized, the sawyer squared tree logs with his broadax to make planks. The carpenter assembled the beams, rafters, walls, and floors of a house, followed by the joiner who added the window moldings, stairs, and wood trim work. Carvers created decorative trim for houses, figureheads for ships, tools, gunstocks, and shop signs. Cabinetmakers crafted furniture, from simple, functional stools and tables to intricate pieces that remain among the finest examples of American craftsmanship.

By the late 1700s, Americans produced much of what they needed, but many goods were still imported. After the Revolutionary War, colonial craftsmen became American craftsmen. For many, their work continued unchanged into the nineteenth century.

PRINTER

The Colonial Williamsburg Foundation

A master
wheelwright
often had an
apprentice.

The Apprentice System

Based on the English model, the apprentice system trained most boys and some girls in a craft that would become their livelihood. At about age fourteen, a youngster was bound over to a master craftsman. A written contract between the child's parents and the master, called an indenture, usually promised that the child would serve the master for seven years, although the length of time could vary. In return, the master promised to teach the new apprentice his trade. The master also was obliged to teach the youngster how to read and write or to allow him to attend evening school to acquire such learning.

The everyday life of the trainee was not easy. Imagine, for example, the apprentice pewterer beginning his day before sunup, stoking the fire in the forge. He would assist his master all day, preparing and preheating molds, and then holding them in the fire while his teacher filled them with melted pewter. When the casting was withdrawn from the mold, the apprentice would help remove any extra bits of metal and smooth the surface of the new plate or pot. The apprentice would then burnish and polish the object. Other daily duties included cleaning the workplace.

When the shop was closed at day's end, the apprentice would eat, and then the master would teach him to read, write, and do sums. Or the master might send the boy to a privately run evening school where he would learn these basic skills as well as some others, such as bookkeeping.

Toward the end of the apprenticeship, the boy would submit an apprentice piece to his master. If this satisfied the master, the latter would sign off on the indenture, and the apprentice would become a journeyman, the next step to becoming a master craftsman. Given a "freedom suit" of new clothes by his master and often a set of tools appropriate to his trade, the fledgling journeyman would set out to find new work and continue his education in the craft.

Making a Pomander

Plimoth Plantation

In the sixteenth century, it became popular to wear small, perforated wooden boxes filled with herbs and spices called pomander boxes. They provided sweet scents that were a welcome relief from unpleasant smells. (Many people wore layers of clothing and rarely washed their clothing or themselves.) Spices and herbs also were believed to protect wearers from disease. Simple apple and orange pomanders were used in the colonies to perfume rooms or cupboards.

Try making your own apple pomander. You can hang it in a closet or place it in a bowl. The pomander will provide a pleasing scent for many months.

You Need

- 1 medium apple
- 2 strips paper (¼ by 12 inches)
- 2 common pins
- 1 ounce whole cloves
- 1 ounce orrisroot powder*
- 2 teaspoons ground cinnamon
- 1 yard colored ribbon ¼ inch wide

- newspaper
- mixing bowl
- wax paper (12 by 12 inches)
- small paper bag

*Orrisroot can be purchased in most health food stores.

Directions

1. Cover your work area with newspaper. Remove the stem from the apple. Use the paper strips to divide the apple into 4 equal sections, crossing the strips at the center top and bottom. Use the pins to hold the strips in place.

2. Insert the cloves into the apple in neat rows, leaving a small space between the cloves.

3. Mix the orrisroot powder and cinnamon in the bowl.

4. Remove the pins and paper strips from the apple. Place the apple in the bowl and completely coat it with powder.

5. Place the apple on the wax paper. Roll the paper around the apple and twist the ends securely. Place the wrapped apple in the paper bag and store it in a cool, dark spot for 1 month.

Plimoth Plantation

6. When the pomander is completely dry, decorate it with the ribbon. Cut the ribbon into two 18-inch pieces. Wrap one piece around the apple and tie it at the center top. Repeat with the second piece. Use the ends of the second piece to make a bow and the ends of the first piece to make a loop that you can use to hang the pomander.

A Hunger for Spices

Sprinkling a bit of pepper on our food is an everyday action. But did you know that pepper and other spices (cloves, nutmeg, allspice, and cinnamon, for example) were once rare and costly? In the Middle Ages, they were considered luxury items from the mysterious Orient. Spices were probably used to cover up the taste of foods that had been preserved in salt or to make spoiled meat more edible.

Spices came from the distant Moluccas (Spice Islands) and India. Trade with the Orient had always been difficult, but it grew more so during the fifteenth century when the Ottoman Turks began to control overland trade routes to India. Their export taxes were so high that a cargo of spices could cost more than eight hundred times the original purchase price in India. Europeans now had an important reason to explore new sea routes to the Far East. In 1498, Vasco da Gama finally reached India by sailing south around Africa. He returned with a cargo of spices and jewels.

The feverish demand for spices resulted in national conflicts as well as great voyages of discovery. Holland and England battled Portugal and each other for control of the spice trade. At the close of the eighteenth century, trade with the Spice Islands was open to all nations, but the popularity of highly spiced foods had waned. For many centuries, however, the hunger for spices had shaped the history of the world.

Freedom Beckons

M ost Africans and their descendents in Colonial America were slaves their entire lives, but slaves sometimes won their freedom. Here are the stories of four who did.

Yarrow Mamout

Philadelphia Museum of Art

Yarrow Mamout

Yarrow Mamout, a Muslim, was born in Africa in the early 1700s. As a young man, he was kidnapped and sold overseas to a Maryland slave owner. Freed by his master's widow when his master died, he worked hard and eventually bought a house and other property near the nation's new capital, in the area known as Georgetown. Mamout lived to be more than 100 years old and followed the teachings of the prophet Muhammad throughout his life.

Oney Judge

Little is known about the early life of Oney Judge, Martha Washington's favorite seamstress. George Washington claimed she was "treated more like a child than a Servant," but Judge was in fact their slave. In 1796, determined to be free, she ran away to Portsmouth, New Hampshire.

Washington tried to have Judge seized and returned. However, when Washington learned that such actions would make him deeply unpopular with the freedom-loving people of New Hampshire, he gave up. In 1797, Judge married John Harris, a free **mulatto** of New Hampshire, and disappeared from the public record.

James Lafayette

Born in Virginia in the late 1740s, James Lafayette was given the name James Armistead, the surname of his owner. In 1781, the Revolutionary War was raging and Armistead

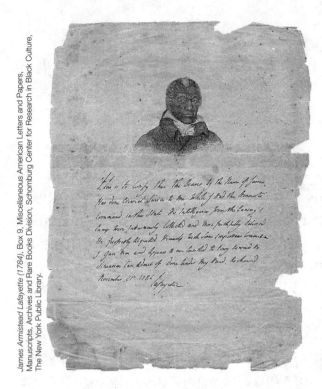

A facsimile of the original certificate from the Marquis de Lafayette commending James Armistead Lafayette for his service as a spy during the Revolutionary War.

Mulatto refers to a person who has one black parent and one white parent.

Marquis de Lafayette, a French general and statesman, served from 1771–1781 in the Continental army in the American Revolution.

volunteered for spy duty under the **Marquis de Lafayette**. Working as a double agent, he provided valuable reports to the patriots that helped them win the war at Yorktown.

At the end of the war, Armistead returned to his master but, in 1786, the Virginia legislature granted him his freedom, thanks in part to a testimonial from Lafayette. Once free, Armistead changed his name to Lafayette. He then bought a farm in Virginia, received a pension for his war service, and died in 1830.

Lucy Terry Prince

Born in West Africa around 1730, Lucy Terry was kidnapped and brought to America as an infant. At age five, she was sold to a settler in the frontier town of Deerfield, Massachusetts. In 1746, she survived an Indian attack and later wrote a poem in memory of the townspeople who died. Ten years later, she married Abijah Prince, a landowner and former slave who purchased her freedom.

The mother of seven children, Prince acquired a reputation for eloquence. She fought for her children's right to a good education and once argued a case before the Vermont Supreme Court. She died in 1821.

The *Franklin Herald* newspaper ran this obituary for Lucy Terry Prince on August 21, 1821.

At Sunderland, Vt. July 11th, Mrs. Lucy Prince, a woman of colour.— From the church and town records where she formerly resided, we learn that she was brought from Bristol, Rhode Island, to Deerfield, Mass. when she was four years old, by Mr. Ebenezer Wells: that she was 97 years of age—that she was early devoted to GOD in Baptism: that she united with the church in Deerfield in 1744—Was married to Abijah Prince, May 17th, 1756, by Elijah Williams, Esq. and that she has been the mother of seven children. In this remarkable woman there was an assemblage of qualities rarely to be found among her sex. Her volubility was exceeded by none, and in general the fluency of her speech captivated all around her, and was not destitute of instruction and edification. She was much respected among her acquaintance. who treated her with a degree of deference.

Vt. Gaz.

Pocumtuck Valley Memorial Library

COLONIAL CURES

Sage

If you were sick in colonial times, who took care of you? What was your treatment? If you had a serious disease like the measles, the doctor came to your house. Dr. John de Sequeyra of Williamsburg treated the measles by "bleeding" you (making a small cut in your skin and letting the blood drip out) and making you *vomit*, or throw up. If your parents had enough money, they paid the doctor. If not, the church paid the doctor's bill.

What if you had a bad headache? In that case, your mother took care of you. She would use a treatment she read in a book or learned from her mother:

> *Put 1 handful of red rose leaves into a pot of vinegar. Boil together till leaves are soft. Add 1 handful of wheat flour. Spread the mixture on the child's clothes and at the sides of the head.*

Rosemary

Imagine you were a slave child with a painful earache. A slave known as a healer might drop warm milk or juice of wormwood into your ear. Slaves often used cures they had known in Africa, changing them to include plants found in New England.

Doctors in colonial days worked hard to make people well, but they did not know that illness was caused by germs.

"Bleeding" was done to reduce swelling, pain, redness, and heat. If a bee stung you on your leg, the doctor would use a *lancet* (a sharp blade) to open a vein close to the swelling. Then he'd let the blood drip into a bowl. If you had a fever from a cold or the flu, the doctor would open a vein on your arm. To bleed delicate areas near the eyes, ears, or mouth, he placed blood-sucking worms called *leeches* on the skin.

Purges also got rid of fluids. There were two kinds of purges, "upward" or "downward." Upward purging was done with a medicine to make you vomit. Downward purging was done with a medicine to make you empty your bowels.

Garlic

Where did these medicines come from? Women grew many of them in their kitchen gardens, plants like garlic, dill, sage, and rosemary. They found other plants in the woods. People also bought medicines from *apothecaries* (a kind of doctor) and druggists. The dried root of a South American plant called *ipecacuanha* (ip-a-kack-kwana) was used to make a person vomit. It is still used today to make a person vomit after swallowing a poison.

So, if you could choose, would you rather be a sick child in colonial times or a sick child today? Having the doctor come to your bedside in colonial times must have been nice. Now you sit in the doctor's waiting room when you don't feel well. Would you rather be made to bleed and vomit after breaking out in a rash, or get a shot to prevent the measles?

Dill

Recently, two leeches from Colonial Williamsburg's Pasteur & Galt Apothecary Shop helped a Virginia doctor reattach a man's ear! (The ear had been cut off in a car accident.) After the operation, the doctor needed to keep the blood moving between the ear and the scalp. He decided to use leeches instead of modern drugs. Leeches can reduce swelling. They improve blood flow by adding blood thinners to break down the local tissues and blood.

An operating room nurse remembered seeing leeches on display at Colonial Williamsburg. The State Police delivered the Williamsburg leeches to the hospital in a glass jar filled with water, with a note that read, "Please return if possible."

By Monica Reiss, *Appleseeds*, © by Carus Publishing Company. Reproduced with permission. Illustrations: © Artville/Getty Images/HIP. Photograph (leech): © Sergey Goruppa/Alamy/HIP. May be reproduced for classroom use. *Toolkit Texts: Short Nonfiction for American History, Colonial Times* by Stephanie Harvey and Anne Goudvis, ©2014 (Portsmouth, NH: Heinemann).

North Wind Picture Archives

FRONTIER LIFE

Colonial America seemed like it had an unending supply of land for settlers. But the first colonies soon became crowded. As more and more people came to America and the population grew, the need for more land for farming also grew. The land in the New England colonies was especially rocky and the soil was thin, making it difficult to grow crops. Colonists began looking to the west for new places to live.

A **domain** is a region or place controlled by a person or group.

Beyond the Mountains

Life for most people in the colonies was centered around the Atlantic Coast. West of this settled area was a vast forested wilderness. It extended across the Appalachian Mountains to the edge of the Great Plains. The only way to travel in those wilds was by foot, horseback, or river craft. Throughout the region, a network of trails had been created over countless centuries by the movement of wildlife and Native Americans. The Indians understandably objected to any advance of colonists into their **domain**.

As colonists moved westward prior to the Revolutionary War, two distinct types of pioneers emerged—

the hunters who led the advance to the frontier, and the farmers who followed. Hunting pioneers depended primarily on wild animals for food. They raised only small crops to supplement their diet. In contrast, farming pioneers depended mainly on crops, hogs, and cows for their food, and they hunted game only to add to that **fare**.

What's for Dinner?

The forest animals that were important for food on the frontier included bear, deer, elk, and woodland bison. Muskets and long rifles were used for hunting. Boys learned to hunt—beginning with small game such as rabbits and squirrels—by the age of ten or twelve.

Although different vegetables were grown, corn was the major crop. It was dried, ground, and mixed with milk or water to make a mush or a type of bread called johnnycake. After the work of clearing trees was done, children took part in planting and weeding. They also helped by keeping animals out of the garden and gathering nuts, berries, and other fruits in the woods.

Home Sweet Home

The typical frontier home was a one-room cabin, usually measuring 12 to 16 feet wide and 16 to 20 feet long. It was built of logs placed horizontally and notched together at the corners. Spaces between the logs were filled with mud and some combination of moss, grass, sticks, and small stones. The pitched roof consisted of layers of overlapping split wood.

Any window openings might be covered with deer hides scraped thin enough to allow in some light. The door and shutters were made of rough-hewn planks and could be locked from the inside. The floors were either simply dirt or fashioned from split logs called puncheons.

Furnishings were sparse and simple. At one end of the cabin stood the structure's most important feature—a large stone fireplace capable of providing both heat and a place for indoor cooking. Children kept

Fare means food and drink.

Isolated living was part of frontier life. Frontier children did their part to help the family survive, including taking care of the livestock.

North Wind Picture Archives

George Rogers Clark: Vincennes Sites Study and Evaluation, George Rogers Clark National Historic Park, Vincennes, Indiana, by Edwin C. Bearss (U.S. Department of the Interior, 1967)

On a white horse, George Rogers Clark confidently leads a group of hardy settlers into the frontier. This is one of 7 murals by Ezra Winter that capture Clark's frontier life.

Illiterate means unable to read and write.

the fireplace supplied with wood from the woodpile, and girls helped with meal preparation.

Colonial Fashion

The materials used for clothing on the frontier included animal skins, a homemade fabric called linsey-woolsey (a combination of linen and wool), and store-bought cloth, such as linen or cotton. Girls learned to sew clothing, making thread on a spinning wheel and weaving cloth on a loom. Men and boys wore jackets, shirts, knee-length breeches, and moccasins. Sometimes, they added leather or thick woolen leggings that might extend halfway up the thigh to protect against snakebites, prickly brush, and cold. Women's and girls' clothing included jackets, dresses, and moccasins. All who lived on the frontier wrapped themselves in bearskins, buffalo hides, or woolen blankets in cold weather.

Growing Up on the Frontier

There was some leisure time on the frontier. When children were not helping their parents, they often ran races, rode horses, went swimming, wrestled, or wandered through the woods. At night, families gathered around the fireplace, and parents told stories of earlier days.

Schools were unavailable on the early frontier, so many of the original pioneers were **illiterate**. As more and more people moved west, however, some settlers began providing schools for their children. Eventually, towns and cities also were established. While life was dangerous, harsh, and difficult on the frontier, it also offered much in the way of freedom and adventure.

Let's Dry Some Apples

Colonial Americans loved apples.
Apples could be eaten fresh, pressed into cider, kept in a root
cellar, cooked into apple butter, or dried to be eaten later.

• • •

The colonists dried apples by laying the slices in the sun.
You can do the same thing with your oven.

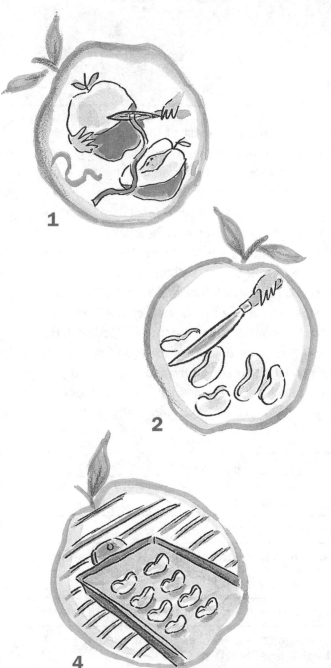

1.

Core and peel the desired
number of apples.
(This might be a step for grown-up help.)

2.

Cut the apples into thin slices.

3.

Turn on the oven to about 120 degrees.

4.

Put a cooling rack onto a cookie sheet
and arrange the apple slices in one layer,
leaving room around each slice.
(If you don't have a cooling rack, you can
put the slices right on the cookie sheet.)

5.

Cook in the oven for approximately
8 to 10 hours. After about 5 hours,
turn the slices over. How do they feel?

6.

Eat and enjoy!
(Any slices that you don't eat should be
stored in a plastic bag in the refrigerator.)

By Anne Austin, *Appleseeds*, © by Carus Publishing Company. Reproduced with permission.
May be reproduced for classroom use. *Toolkit Texts: Short Nonfiction for American History, Colonial Times*
by Stephanie Harvey and Anne Goudvis, ©2014 (Portsmouth, NH: Heinemann).

No Fridge? No Problem!

In colonial times, families produced most of their food on their farm and had to preserve it for use throughout the year. Crops grown in the summer and fall had to be saved for the long winter and spring. But there were no refrigerators like we have today. So how did colonial housewives keep food from spoiling without refrigerators or freezers? Most homes had a root cellar or other type of cold storage place. These were usually cellars underneath their houses or other small underground places. Food could also be kept cold by lowering it into a well or spring, setting containers right in the cold water. Straw could be used to insulate food and keep it cold. Wealthy people might build ice houses, where huge blocks of ice cut from ponds in the winter could be packed in sawdust and used to keep food cold. Housewives also used salt to preserve meat and vegetables, and sometimes pickled food in vinegar. Meat could be preserved by smoking it with the smoke of a green fire. Other foods, such as vegetables, apples and other fruits, beans, and even meat jerky or fish, could be preserved by drying them in the sun.

COLONIAL FOOD	HOW TO PRESERVE IT
Beans	Salted, pickled, or dried
Beverages (beer, ale, wine, cider)	Stored in cellar or coolest part of house
Butter	Covered with salt (had to soak before eating to remove salt)
Eggs	Kept in a cool place or pickled
Ice cream	Could not be stored. A rare treat to be eaten right away!
Meat and fish	Salted, canned, potted (cooked, then packed in a jar and coated with a layer of fat), or dried
Milk	Made into cheese and coated with wax to preserve it

No Ordinary Shells

A wood engraving of William Penn's treaty with Native Americans in Pennsylvania in the 1680s. A wampum belt was given to Penn to commemorate the treaty.

The ancient saying that the whole is equal to more than the sum of its parts fits wampum perfectly. A single small wampum bead does not look like much. But the Indians of the Northeast wove thousands of beads into pictographic belts that record major events in American Indian and colonial history during the seventeenth and eighteenth centuries. The surviving belts are regarded today as important American historical documents and are carefully guarded by Indians and museums in the United States, Canada, and Europe.

By Stanley A. Freed, *Cobblestone*, © by Carus Publishing Company. Reproduced with permission. May be reproduced for classroom use. *Toolkit Texts: Short Nonfiction for American History, Colonial Times* by Stephanie Harvey and Anne Goudvis, ©2014 (Portsmouth, NH: Heinemann).

Ceremonial Tokens

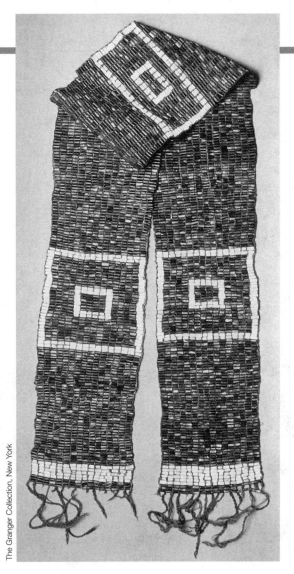

An Iroquois wampum belt

Belts are only part of the history of wampum, which goes back to prehistoric times, long before the beginning of the colonial period. Beads in the shape of thin disks with a hole in the center, made mostly from the shells of the quahog clam, have been found at many archaeological sites. The beads come in two colors, white and purple. Purple beads are more valuable because the purple area of a shell is smaller than the white part. Since the disk-shaped beads were thin, drilling the center hole was rather simple, even with the stone tools that were in use before Europeans introduced iron. American Indians used these beads for decoration, for gifts on ceremonial occasions, as invitations to ceremonies, as tokens to console people who were grieving the loss of a loved one, and for the commemoration of important agreements.

Pocket Change

When European settlers arrived along the coast of northeastern America in the early seventeenth century, they had some conflicts with the native peoples they encountered, but the two peoples also traded with each other. Wampum helped to oil the wheels of commerce. It was small, light, and easy to carry, features that made it useful as money. Fur traders dealing with Indians began using wampum in this way. As it became more commonplace as currency, laws were passed to fix its value.

A wampum strand

The typical wampum bead of colonial times was a smooth cylinder averaging about a quarter of an inch in length and an eighth of an inch in diameter. The lengthwise hole was made with an iron drill. The process was simple, but it required considerable skill because the clamshell is hard and brittle and the beads are narrow. Finished beads were made into strings about a foot long. Five to ten strings, each worth twelve and a half cents, were a good day's work.

Wampum was taken to Europe, where it was copied in porcelain. The Indians liked the glass beads and they were cheaper. Consequently, wampum lost its value as currency and was no longer needed. Today "wampum" is simply a dated slang word for money.

Symbols of History

Wampum belts, however, have remained an important part of American Indian history. The belts have designs made by contrasting purple and white beads. The designs usually commemorate treaties, contracts, or other agreements. For example, one wampum belt more than six feet long has the design of an Iroquois longhouse at the center, flanked by two figures representing Iroquois. Thirteen other figures representing the thirteen original American colonies are arranged on either side of the Iroquois. The figures are all holding hands. The belt commemorates a peace pact between the colonies and the League of the Iroquois.

Copyright © 2013 Florida Center for Instructional Technology

The wampum belt given to William Penn.

The designs on wampum belts are not writing but symbols, which serve as memory aids. The events and agreements associated with wampum belts were much too complicated to be documented adequately by a few symbols. Specialists memorized the meaning of wampum belts and taught the text associated with each belt to their successors. These specialists were like living libraries. They could recite long accounts of important matters while running their fingers lightly over the belts. The meaning of some wampum belts is known today, but the stories represented by many others have been forgotten.

The New World

Library of Congress

The *Mayflower* left England in September 1620 with 102 passengers. Half of these passengers were known as Separatists or Saints—people who wanted a complete separation from the Church of England. Traveling with them were the Strangers—hired men, servants, and others, who wanted to start a new life in a new land. Today, the Separatists and the Strangers of the *Mayflower* are known as the Pilgrims.

After the Saints and Strangers arrived on the shores of North America, it took more than a month for them to find a place to settle. Here is their account of that time, beginning with the landfall at Cape Harbor.

Above: John Alden was probably the first Pilgrim to step ashore at Plymouth Harbor. This painting shows a Pilgrim giving thanks after the long voyage.

November 11th. We came to an anchor in the bay, which is a good harbor and pleasant bay about four miles over from land to land, wherein a thousand sail of ships may safely ride.

And every day we saw whales playing hard by us in that place. Had we had instruments and means to take them (which to our great grief we wanted) we might have made a very rich return.

We could not come near the shore by three quarters of an English mile because of shallow water. This was a great prejudice to us, for our people going on shore were forced to wade a bowshot or two in going a-land, which caused many to get colds and coughs, for it was freezing weather.

Excerpts from *Homes in the Wilderness: A Pilgrim's Journal of Plymouth Plantation in 1620* by William Bradford and Others. Edited by Margaret Wise Brown and published by Linnet Books, the children's imprint of The Shoe String Press, Inc., 925 Sherman Avenue, Hamden, CT 06514. Available in cloth and paper bindings. From *Cobblestone,* © by Carus Publishing Company. Reproduced with permission. May be reproduced for classroom use. *Toolkit Texts: Short Nonfiction for American History, Colonial Times* by Stephanie Harvey and Anne Goudvis, ©2014 (Portsmouth, NH: Heinemann).

> ## Our people went on shore to refresh themselves and our women to wash, as they had great need.

November 13th. Monday, we unshipped our shallop (a small boat used for fishing) and drew her on land to mend and repair her, having been forced to cut her down in bestowing her betwixt the decks. She was much opened with the people's lying in her, which kept us long there, for our carpenter made slow work of it. It was sixteen or seventeen days before he had finished her. Our people went on shore to refresh themselves and our women to wash, as they had great need.

While men worked to repair the shallop and most of the passengers continued to live on the Mayflower, *a small party of men set out to explore the land to discover a place that would be good for settlement. Such a place would have to offer "a convenient harbor . . . good corn ground . . . good fishing" and be "healthful, secure, and defensible."*

Sixteen men explored on foot, discovering native corn fields, abandoned home sites, and "springs of fresh water, of which were heartily glad, and sat us down and drank our first New England water with as much delight as ever we had drunk in our lives." A most helpful discovery was mounds of corn buried by natives for winter storage. The explorers took what they could carry back to the Mayflower, *where the food supply was running out, and vowed to repay the natives when they got a chance.*

When the shallop was repaired, more explorations began by boat along the shoreline of Cape Cod. It was December 6 when the final party "set out in very cold and hard weather." The party landed in a small bay that night, and the next morning, half the group set out to explore the area, with the rest staying behind to guard the shallop.

That day they followed Indian tracks and found "a great burying place," "more corn ground," and "four or five Indian houses which had been lately dwelt in." The explorers slept ashore that night.

About midnight we heard a great and hideous cry, and our sentinel called *Arm, Arm.* So we bestirred ourselves and shot off a couple of muskets, and the noise ceased. We concluded that it was a company of wolves or foxes, for one told us he heard such a noise in New-found-land.

December 8th. About five o'clock in the morning we began stirring, and two or three who doubted whether their pieces would go off or no made trial of them and shot them off, but thought nothing of it. After prayer we prepared ourselves for breakfast and for a journey, and it being now the twilight in the morning, it was thought meet to carry the things down to the shallop.

Anon, all of a sudden, we heard a great and strange cry, which we knew to be the same voices, though they varied their notes. One of our company being abroad came running in and cried, *They are men! Indians! Indians!* And withal, their arrows came flying amongst us.

Our men ran out with all speed to recover their arms, as by the good providence of God they did. In the meantime, Captain Miles Standish, having a snaphance ready, made a shot. Another shot after him. After they two had shot, another two of us were ready, but he wished us not to shoot until we could take aim, for we knew not what need we should have. There were only four who had their arms ready. We stood before the open side of our barricade which was assaulted, for we thought it best to defend it lest the enemy should take it and our stuff and so have the more vantage against us.

The cry of our enemies was dreadful, especially when our men ran out to recover their arms. Their note was after this manner, *Woath woach ha ha hach woach.* Our men were no sooner in arms but the enemy was ready to assault them. There was a lusty man and no whit less valiant, who was thought to be their captain and who stood behind a tree within half a musket shot of us and there let his arrows fly at us. He was seen to shoot three arrows which were all avoided. He at whom the first arrow was aimed saw it and stood down and it flew over him. The rest were avoided also. He stood three shots of a musket, but at length one took full aim at him, after which he gave an extraordinary cry and away they went all.

We followed them about a quarter of a mile, leaving six to keep our shallop, for we were careful of our business. Then we shouted all together two several times and shot off a couple of muskets and so returned. This we did that they might see we were not afraid of them nor discouraged.

Thus it pleased God to vanquish our enemies and give us deliverance. By their noise we could guess that they were not less than thirty or forty. . . . So after we had given God thanks for our deliverance, we took our shallop and went on our journey. We called this place the first encounter. From hence we intended to have sailed the afore said Thievish Harbor, if we found no convenient harbor by the way. Having the wind good, we sailed all the day along the coast about fifteen leagues

One tradition holds that Mary Chilton was the first woman among the Pilgrims to come ashore, stepping onto the rock that served as a useful landing place.

North Wind Picture Archives

English Puritan settlers arriving on the winter shores of Cape Cod.

but saw neither river nor creek to put into. After we sailed an hour or two, it began to snow and rain and to be bad weather. About the midst of the afternoon the wind increased and the seas began to be very rough. The hinges of the rudder broke, so that we could steer no longer with it, but two men with much ado were fain to serve with a couple of oars. The seas were grown so great that we were much troubled and in great danger, and night grew on.

Anon Master Coppin bade us be of good cheer for he saw the harbor. As we drew near, the gale being stiff and we bearing great sail to get in, we split our mast in three pieces and were like to have cast away our shallop. Yet by God's mercy recovering ourselves, we had the flood with us and struck into the harbor.

Now he that thought this had been the place was deceived, for it was a place where not any of us had been before. Coming into the harbor he that was our pilot did bear up, which had

cast us away if he had continued. Yet still the Lord kept us, for we bore up toward an island before us, and gained the lee of this island. Being compassed about with many rocks and dark night growing upon us, it pleased the divine providence that we fell upon a place of sandy ground upon a strange island, where our shallop did ride safe and secure all that night. We kept our watch all night in that rain upon that island.

December 9th. In the morning we marched about it and found no inhabitants at all.

December 11th. On Monday we sounded the harbor and found it a very good harbor for our shipping. We marched also into the land and found divers corn fields and little running brooks, a place very good for situation. So we returned to our ship again with the good news to the rest of our people, which did much to comfort their hearts.

MUTINY

Plimoth Plantation

on the *Mayflower*

The day after the Pilgrims sighted land, a mutiny broke out on the *Mayflower*. William Bradford, in his history *Of Plymouth Plantation*, describes what took place. Some Strangers on board, he says, "began making discontented and mutinous speeches," claiming that when they came ashore, "they would use their own liberty . . . for none had power to command them." From this conflict came a document that later helped set the stage for democratic government in the United States.

People think of the Pilgrims as a tightly knit band of like-minded people seeking a place to worship as they saw fit. Actually, the passengers were a diverse group. Fewer than half were religious Separatists: people who wanted a complete separation from the Church of England; the others were people Bradford called Strangers: freemen, indentured servants, and hired hands looking to start a new life in a new land. Given the cramped quarters on the *Mayflower* and the length of the voyage, it is not surprising that conflicts broke out.

The Strangers, who claimed that "none had power to command them," were technically correct. The group's *patent*, or permission to settle, was from the Virginia Company. The Pilgrims, however, came to Cape Cod an area outside that company's jurisdiction. Once on shore, the Strangers could indeed do as they pleased.

The conflict highlighted a sober fact: Life in the wilderness was demanding, and the group needed the help of everyone on board in order to survive. So someone (Bradford does not say who) drew up a common agreement. This extraordinary document states, "We whose names are underwritten . . . solemnly and mutually in the presence of God, and of one another, Covenant and Combine ourselves together in a Civil Body Politic . . . to enact, constitute, and frame such just and equal Laws, . . . as shall be thought meet and convenient for the general good of the Colony."

The seeds of the agreement lie in the religious views of the Separatists. Their belief that each church congregation should elect its own officers in a democratic manner led to the notion of a democratic covenant in political life as well.

On November 21, 1620, the agreement was signed aboard ship. The original document has disappeared, but Edward Winslow and William Bradford included a copy in an early account of the colony called *Mourt's Relation*. Bradford also wrote about both the mutiny and the agreement in his history. Bradford's history disappeared

during the Revolutionary War. Years later, it turned up in London and was returned to the United States. Over the years, Americans "rediscovered" the *Mayflower* agreement as the important document it is. They began to call it the Mayflower Compact because they saw it as an example of the type of "social compact" philosophers of the time considered necessary for good government.

The compact did not establish democracy as people think of it today. For instance, not everyone on board was asked to sign: Women and some indentured servants were excluded. But the *idea* it expressed—that the power to govern comes from the people—is the same as that on which American democracy is based. Thus, long before Thomas Jefferson wrote that governments derive their power from the consent of the governed, a group of weary passengers determined that they would join "together in a Civil Body Politic" in order to frame "just and equal Laws."

This engraving by Gauthier (after a painting by T. H. Matteson) depicts the signing of The Mayflower Compact, the social contract to establish basic law and order in the colony.

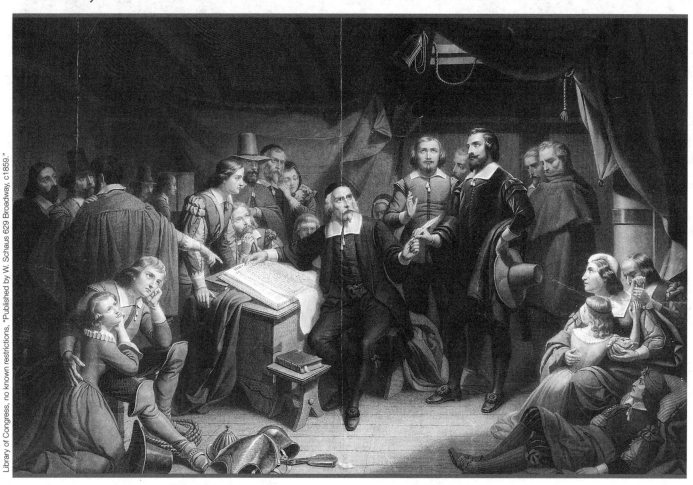

By Ellen Donohue Warwick, *Cobblestone*, © by Carus Publishing Company. Reproduced with permission. May be reproduced for classroom use. *Toolkit Texts: Short Nonfiction for American History, Colonial Times* by Stephanie Harvey and Anne Goudvis, ©2014 (Portsmouth, NH: Heinemann).

An Agreement of Trust

For the Pilgrims, the winter of 1620–1621 was grim. Although there was little snow or frost, the cold, wet weather wore them down. Food supplies diminished. By spring, the Pilgrims had not tasted fresh fruits or vegetables for four months. Half the population of Plymouth lay buried on Cole's Hill. Only twenty-two of the thirty-eight grown men survived the winter. The women fared even worse. The settlers remembered all too well their first encounter with the Nauset Wampanoag on Cape Cod. To hide their weakened state from them, the Pilgrims buried their dead by night in unmarked graves.

Welcoming Newcomers

The Pilgrims were especially fearful one day when an Indian entered the settlement. Saluting them, he said, "Welcome, Englishmen." He explained to the astonished people that he was Samoset, an Abenaki from what is now Maine, and had learned English from men on trading and fishing boats along the coast. Throughout the evening, Samoset provided the Pilgrims with information about the area. Plymouth, he explained, was

On March 16, 1621, Samoset startled the Pilgrims when he walked into their settlement.

The Wampanoags were farmers but also got food by fishing, hunting, and gathering wild foods. Their village life is re-created at Plimoth Plantation.

the site of a Wampanoag village called Patuxet, which a plague had wiped out a few years earlier. Samoset told the Pilgrims the names of nearby Wampanoag communities, their size, and the names of their sachems, or leaders. One of the closet communities was the Pokanoket Wampanoag, who lived to the west. Their sachem was Ousamequin (Yellow Feather), also known as Massasoit (respected leader).

A few days later Samoset returned with another Indian. To the Pilgrims' amazement, this man also spoke English. Tisquantum, or Squanto as he was called, had been kidnapped by Englishmen exploring the coast and sold to Spaniards as a slave. After several years in Spain, Squanto was taken to England, where he learned English. Squanto then served as an interpreter for an English expedition to North America. Returning to his native Patuxet, Squanto found his home deserted. By 1621, he was living with Massasoit's community.

Years later, Governor Bradford would call Squanto "a speciall instrumente sent of God for their good beyond their expectation." But in 1621, he and Samoset led Massasoit and sixty warriors into Plymouth. Would the chief use his power to destroy the struggling settlement?

By Karen E. Hong, *Cobblestone,* © by Carus Publishing Company. Reproduced with permission.
May be reproduced for classroom use. *Toolkit Texts: Short Nonfiction for American History, Colonial Times*
by Stephanie Harvey and Anne Goudvis, ©2014 (Portsmouth, NH: Heinemann).

FORGING AN AGREEMENT

Conscious that they had settled on foreign land, the Pilgrims welcomed Massasoit with respect. Edward Winslow presented him with a gift of knives and a chain with a jewel in it. The men invited Massasoit to enter an house, and after seating him on cushions Governor Carver offered him drink and food. With Squanto as interpreter, the governor and the sachem reached a diplomatic agreement that benefitted both sides.

The Wampanoag and Pilgrims agreed they would not injure each other. Offenders would be punished by the victim's people. If one group was attacked, the other would come to its defense. As part of the treaty, the Wampanoag and Pilgrims would not carry weapons when visiting each other. As a result, Massasoit gained an ally against the Wampanoags' enemies, the powerful Narragansetts, and the Pilgrims had less fear of being attacked. This treaty would last more than fifty years until after Massasoit's death.

Although the other Indians soon departed from Plymouth, Squanto remained with the Pilgrims. He taught the settlers skills that were vital to survival in their new land: where to fish, how to catch eels, where to catch herring for use as food and fertilizer, and how to grow corn. Squanto became the Pilgrims' interpreter and guide. Massasoit later sent another Wampanoag man, Hobbamock, as his representative to Plymouth Colony.

LENDING ASSISTANCE

Only a few months passed before Governor Bradford sought Massasoit's aid. Young John Billington became lost while wandering in the woods. When five days passed without the boy being found, Bradford asked Massasoit for help. Massasoit learned that John had been found and taken to the Nauset community of Wampanoag on Cape Cod. Bradford sent men to bring him home.

Almost immediately, the Pilgrims were able to return the favor. When they learned through Squanto that the Narragansett were trying to drive Massasoit from his land and turn his people against him, Myles Standish and other settlers warned the Narragansetts that Massasoit must be allowed to return to his land unharmed. The threat succeeded, and Massasoit maintained his position.

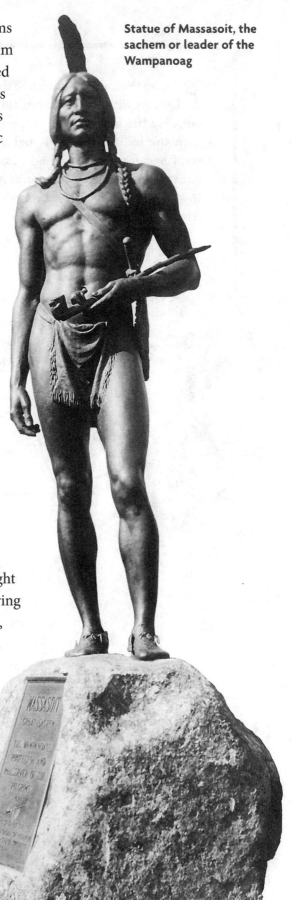

Statue of Massasoit, the sachem or leader of the Wampanoag

Left and right: *Dictionary of American Portraits*, Dover Publications, Inc., 1967

Edward Winslow, *right*, joined the Pilgrim congregation in Leyden. His wife, Elizabeth, sailed with him to America but died the first winter. Winslow was active in contacts with the Indians, including helping Massasoit when the chief became ill. He married Susannah White in 1621 and became an assistant governor in 1625. He left Plymouth in 1644 to serve with Oliver Cromwell in the West Indies and died before he could return.

William Bradford, *left*, was 16 when he left England for Amsterdam. He crossed to America with his wife, Dorothy, and was one of the exploring party that discovered Plymouth Harbor. After the death of Governor John Carver, Bradford was elected to govern the colony in 1621 and was reelected each year until his death in 1656, except for five years when he was asked not to serve. A well-read man, he became New England's first historian when he wrote his history of Plymouth Colony, *Of Plymouth Plantation*.

The Pilgrims received threats as well as gave them. In January 1622, Canonicus, leader of the Narragansett, sent Governor Bradford a snakeskin wrapped around a bundle of arrows. The settlers interpreted it as a challenge to fight. After removing the arrows, Bradford filled the skin with bullets and returned it to Canonicus. Alarmed by weapons he'd not seen before, Canonicus refused to be near the returned snakeskin, causing it to be passed from Indian to Indian and finally back to Plymouth.

ESTABLISHING AN ENDURING FRIENDSHIP

Despite threats by other Native communities, the treaty between Massasoit and the colonists endured. In September 1621, several other sachems signed it. The relationship helped protect the Pilgrims and provided them with food during lean times.

Threatened with starvation in 1622, the Pilgrims decided to trade the Indians glass beads and other trade goods for corn. Squanto led Governor

Bradford and his men to Cape Cod to buy food, but Squanto died on the journey. Hobbamock,who had been living in Plymouth, took his place as guide and helper to the Pilgrims.

The friends grew closer in March 1623. Word reached Governor Bradford that Massasoit was sick, possibly even dying, and wished to see his friend Edward Winslow. When Winslow, accompanied by Hobbamock, reached Massasoit, he diagnosed the problem and administered medication. Winslow stayed at Massasoit's side until he was restored to health. Grateful for Winslow's attention, Massasoit warned him that the Narragansett were joining with others to attack first a colony newly settled at Weymouth and then Plymouth. Massasoit's warning allowed Myles Standish to move against those organizing the attacks and thwart their plans.

Despite the challenges the Pilgrims faced, their good relations with Massasoit and other Wampanoag people helped their colony survive.

Artifacts from the 17th-century Wampanoags are preserved at Plimoth Plantation.

Plimoth Plantation

Mary Rowlandson

"It was the dolefulest day that ever mine eyes saw"

This is how Mary Rowlandson described the day in February of 1675 when the Native American forces of King Philip attacked the town of Lancaster, Massachusetts. Mary and her three young children were inside their garrison house. Because of the threat of attack, these were houses that had been specially designed to protect families, with thick log or plank walls. At this time there was a war going on between the colonial families and King Philip's forces. King Philip (whose real name was Metacomet) was Chief Massasoit's son and now a Native American leader of the Wampanoag tribe in New England. The colonists were settling in more and more of the territories that had belonged to native tribes. Soon these tribes were attacking colonial settlements and killing settlers. Eventually the colonists would declare war against the native tribes. It would be called King Philip's War or the First Indian War.

The colonial settlers who were living in Lancaster were always prepared for an attack. Families were ready to take refuge in the garrison houses, like the Rowlandson's, if necessary. On that February morning, thirty-seven people crowded into Mary's home

A wood engraving of Mary White Rowlandson, in a canoe, being held captive by Native Americans.

for protection. Because Mary later wrote a book about the attack and what happened to her afterwards, we have an account of the day, and what happened afterwards, in her own words.

"On the tenth of February 1675, came the Indians with great numbers upon Lancaster: their first coming was about sunrising; hearing the noise of some guns, we looked out; several houses were burning, and the smoke ascending to heaven," Mary wrote. Soon those inside the house smelled smoke. The Native American warriors had set fire to Rowlandson's house, forcing everyone inside to come out. Many of them were killed instantly. Mary was shot in the side and her six year old daughter was injured. 13 settlers were killed and 24, including Mary and her three children, were taken captive by King Philip's warriors. "I had often before this said that if the Indians should come, I should choose rather to be killed by them than taken alive, but when it came to the trial my mind changed; their glittering weapons so daunted my spirit, that I chose rather to go along with [them], than that moment to end my days," Mary later admitted.

Mary was held captive by King Philip and the Wampanoag for 11 weeks. She finally healed the wound in her side by packing it with oak leaves as a bandage. Her daughter Sarah died, and her other two children were held by another tribe. Mary was forced to stay with the tribe as it moved through what is now southwestern New Hampshire and Vermont, fleeing the colonial militia soldiers. Conditions were harsh. Mary was sore and cold and had very little

The release of Mary Rowlandson from her captors was negotiated atop a granite ledge, later named Redemption Rock.

1630 1930

REDEMPTION ROCK

UPON THE ROCK FIFTY FEET WEST OF THIS SPOT MARY ROWLANDSON, WIFE OF THE FIRST MINISTER OF LANCASTER, WAS REDEEMED FROM CAPTIVITY UNDER KING PHILIP. THE NARRATIVE OF HER EXPERIENCE IS ONE OF THE CLASSICS OF COLONIAL LITERATURE.

MASSACHUSETTS BAY COLONY TERCENTENARY COMMISSION

Photos left and right by David Stirling

to eat. "The first week of my being among them I hardly ate anything; the second week I found my stomach grow very faint for want of something; and yet it was very hard to get down their filthy trash; but the third week, though I could think how formerly my stomach would turn against this or that, and I could starve and die before I could eat such things, yet they were sweet and savory to my taste," Mary wrote. She ate things like acorns, roots, wild birds, the ears and entrails of horses, and even frogs, skunks, and the bark from trees.

Mary stayed with the tribe as it fled from the colonial soldiers. She sewed clothing for members of the tribe and sold them for food or a knife. Sometimes Mary was treated with kindness and offered food and a warm place to sit. Other times she was ignored, left to sit in the cold and faint from hunger. She witnessed many attacks on the colonial settlements. "I was with the enemy eleven weeks and five days," she remembered, "and not one week passed without the fury of the [tribe], and some desolation by fire and sword upon one place or other."

Finally the tribe made its way back into Massachusetts. Mary hoped that she would be ransomed, meaning that money would be paid to the tribe in exchange for her freedom. A group of women in Boston raised the money (20 English pounds) and a man named John Hoar brought the money to a place called Redemption Rock in Princeton, Massachusetts. "So I took my leave of them, and in coming along my heart melted into tears, more than all the while I was with them, and I was almost swallowed up with the thoughts that ever I should go home again," Mary wrote. On May 2, 1676, Mary Rowlandson was free once more. She was reunited with her husband and surviving children.

Many colonial settlers had experiences like Mary's when they were captured by King Philip's warriors. But what sets Mary's story apart is that she later wrote a book about what happened to her. *The Narrative of the Captivity and the Restoration of Mrs. Mary Rowlandson* was published in Boston in 1682. It tells Mary's story in her own words and became the first "best seller" in American history. King Philip's War ended in 1677, a year after Metacomet himself was killed by colonists. The Native American tribes could no longer stop the expansion of colonial settlers into their territories.

The title page of Mary Rowlandson's *A Narrative of the Captivity, Sufferings, and Removes of Mrs. Mary Rowlandson.*

PHILLIS WHEATLEY
The Mother of American Poetry

Characters

Phillis Wheatley
an African slave
brought to
Massachusetts

John Wheatley
a prosperous
white tailor
from Boston

Susannah Wheatley
the wife of
John Wheatley

Mary Wheatley
the daughter of
John and Susannah
Wheatley

Narrator 1

Narrator 2

By Charles F. Baker, illustrated by Mark Mitchell, *Footprints*, © by Carus Publishing Company. Reproduced with permission.
May be reproduced for classroom use. *Toolkit Texts: Short Nonfiction for American History, Colonial Times*
by Stephanie Harvey and Anne Goudvis, ©2014 (Portsmouth, NH: Heinemann).

Introduction

Narrator 1: When a young African girl was purchased as a slave by the Wheatley family in Boston, the Wheatleys quickly realized that she was bright and curious. Before long, the girl, whom they had named Phillis, was being educated by the Wheatleys' daughter, Mary, and writing her own poems. She went on to become the first black person, the first slave, and the second woman in America to publish a book of poems.

Act 1, Scene 1

Narrator 2: The Wheatley home in Boston in 1761. Susannah Wheatley, the mistress of the house, has just returned from the slave market, where she bought a young African girl for the household. Susannah has been looking for a young slave to replace some of her older servants. She also wants a companion to care for her in her old age. Susannah sends the young slave girl to the servants' quarters to be bathed, clothed, and fed. She enters the parlor, where her husband and daughter are reading before the fire, to tell them of her recent purchase.

Susannah Wheatley: I found a new girl in the slave market today.

Mary Wheatley *(looking up from her book)*: How old is she?

Susannah: About seven or eight years old, I think.

Mary: Oh, good! Mother, may I name her?

Susannah: Yes, my dear, you may.

Mary: I have always liked the name Phillis, and it's the name of the ship that brought her here. I think Phillis Wheatley goes well together. Don't you, Father?

John Wheatley: Yes, Mary, it does. *(turning to his wife)* Is she healthy?

Susannah: Not in appearance. She is very thin and obviously suffering from the long trip from Africa. The conditions on slave ships are so terrible. It is a wonder that any of them make it here alive. Just the extreme change of climate is enough to do them in. She was naked except for a dirty piece of carpet wrapped around her. She also recently lost her front teeth. That is why I think she is about seven or eight years old.

John: Why did you choose her, if she is not healthy? We do not need a sick servant who is unable to do any work.

Susannah: It was the intelligent expression on her face that attracted me to her. She had such a thoughtful look.

Mary: I am eager to meet Phillis.

Susannah: You may when she has rested. The poor girl is frightened and exhausted.

Narrator 2: Mary impatiently returns to the book she is reading, while her parents continue to discuss other household matters.

Act 1, Scene 2

Narrator 1: *The Wheatley home 16 months later. Susannah soon realizes that she has bought an extraordinary girl with a sharp mind. Phillis is not trained as a domestic as it was first intended, and she is not allowed to associate with the other servants in the household. She is kept constantly in the company of her mistress and Mary. Susannah and Phillis are spending a quiet afternoon in the library.*

Susannah: Phillis, are you cold? I am worried about the effect of this damp weather on your delicate health.

Phillis Wheatley: No, Mistress Wheatley. The wool shawl you gave me and the fire are keeping me plenty warm.

Susannah: I am still amazed at how well you speak English. You have been with us only 16 months!

Mary *(proudly looking at her pupil, who lowers her head humbly)*: And she can read well, too.

Susannah: I know. I told our neighbors that Phillis could read the sacred writings of the Bible, but they did not believe me. I had to bring them in and prove it to them. They were astonished.

Mary: She also has been learning to write since I had her put the alphabet on the wall with a piece of chalk. Now we practice every day with chalk or charcoal.

Susannah: What subjects are you learning now, Phillis?

Phillis: Mary has started to teach me about astronomy, geography, and literature. I want to learn about everything.

Susannah: Why is that?

Phillis: I am just curious, I guess.

Susannah: That's a good enough reason. What do you enjoy learning the most?

Phillis: I like words and the way different ones sound. I like to put them together so that they have special meaning.

Susannah: Maybe someday you will write poetry.

Phillis: What is poetry?

Susannah: You will learn, Phillis. You will learn.

Narrator 2: The two girls continue studying as Susannah sits watching them contently.

Phillis's poor health does not keep her from her studies, which continue over the years under the direction of Mary and some of her friends. When she is 14 years old, Phillis writes her first poem—"To the University of Cambridge in New England"—in which she advises disobedient college boys to avoid sin and follow Christ. Phillis continues to write poems, and she soon becomes widely known.

Act 1, Scene 3

Narrator 1: The Wheatley home on a Sunday afternoon in August 1772. The cold, damp New England weather has affected Phillis's fragile health. She has asthma, and to help her condition, the Wheatleys send her to the country during the week. She returns to the city to spend every Sunday with the family. Over dinner, John, Susannah, and Mary Wheatley discuss with Phillis the progress of her studies and her future.

John: Phillis, Mary has told me that you have been learning Latin. How have you done with it?

Phillis: Very well, sir. I have been fortunate to have tutors like Mary and her friends, who have been able to teach me so many subjects.

John: What subjects have you been studying and reading about lately?

Phillis: I have been studying Christian scripture, ancient history, and mythology.

John: You obviously love to learn. What do you enjoy most?

Phillis: I like to read the classics, especially Virgil, Ovid, and Horace. I also have enjoyed the writings of Milton, Gray, Addison, and Isaac Watts. I like the literature of Pope very much, and I especially love his translation of Homer.

John: Why is that?

Phillis: I use his meter and rhyme in most of my verse when I write poetry.

John *(very impressed)*: You are getting the equal of a college education. (turning to his daughter) Mary, I am pleased with the quality and the quantity of education you have given Phillis. Her poetry shows your efforts.

Mary: Thank you, Father. I must admit that she has learned much on her own.

Susannah: I have placed a lamp and writing material on a table beside Phillis's bed in case she should have any thoughts at night. That way she can write them down without having to get up and go to her desk in the cold. Her health is so delicate.

Phillis: Thank you, Mistress Wheatley. I often have ideas that would flee by dawn if I were not to write them down before I rose.

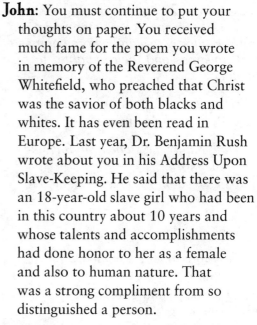

John: You must continue to put your thoughts on paper. You received much fame for the poem you wrote in memory of the Reverend George Whitefield, who preached that Christ was the savior of both blacks and whites. It has even been read in Europe. Last year, Dr. Benjamin Rush wrote about you in his Address Upon Slave-Keeping. He said that there was an 18-year-old slave girl who had been in this country about 10 years and whose talents and accomplishments had done honor to her as a female and also to human nature. That was a strong compliment from so distinguished a person.

Phillis: Yes, sir. I was pleased to read that.

John: What poem are you writing now?

Phillis: I have been following the political events in the colonies with great enthusiasm. I have written a poem that makes a statement about the black patriot's position.

John: How are you going to present this noble and worthy statement?

Phillis: This month, the earl of Dartmouth was appointed as secretary of state for our colonies. This is a good sign for the end of British tyranny [absolute control] in America. The earl was a good friend of Reverend Whitefield, who, as you know, believes in fairness for all people. He is also friendly with the countess of Huntingdon, who is against slavery. I want to welcome the earl with a patriotic message from our land.

John: May we hear this new poem of yours?

Susannah: Yes, Phillis, read your poem to us.

Phillis *(proudly)*: I will be happy to read it to you.

By Charles F. Baker, illustrated by Mark Mitchell, *Footprints*, © by Carus Publishing Company. Reproduced with permission. May be reproduced for classroom use. *Toolkit Texts: Short Nonfiction for American History, Colonial Times* by Stephanie Harvey and Anne Goudvis, ©2014 (Portsmouth, NH: Heinemann).

Narrator 2: *Phillis goes to her room to get her recently completed poem. She returns shortly to stand before her master and mistress and their daughter to read it aloud.*

Phillis: I greet the earl of Dartmouth with my opening lines:

Hail, happy day, when, smiling like the morn,
Fair Freedom rose New-England to adorn.

I then go on:

No more America, in mournful strain
Of wrongs, and grievance unredress'd complain,
No longer shall thou dread the iron chain,
Which wanton Tyranny with lawless hand
Had made, and with it meant t'enslave the land.

The key words in those lines are "America," "Tyranny," and "t'enslave." They lead to the next stanza, which makes a statement on one side of black patriotism:

Should you, my lord, while you peruse my song,
Wonder from whence my love of Freedom sprung,
Whence flow these wishes for the common good,
By feeling hearts alone best understood,
I, young in life, by seeming cruel fate
Was snatch'd from Afric's fancy'd happy seat:
What pangs excruciating must molest,
What sorrows labour in my parent's breast?
Steel'd was that soul and by no misery mov'd
That from a father seiz'd his babe belov'd:

And I end the stanza with:

Such, such my case. And can I then but pray
Others may never feel tyrannic sway?

Narrator 2: John, Susannah, and Mary applaud the performance. Phillis beams with pride and pleasure at the approval of her patrons.

John: That was moving, Phillis. I am sure the earl will be impressed by your efforts and affected by your message. Have you ever thought to put your poems into a book? I think that such a venture would meet with much success. Your poems are so widely read and admired now.

Phillis: Yes, sir. I have wanted to publish my poems collectively. I have already put together a manuscript of almost 40 poems. All I need now is one to begin the book—an ode that will thank you for all you have given to me and a statement that declares that I am a black poet.

John: I am very happy to hear that you have already compiled your poems into a manuscript for publication. When you complete the beginning ode, give them all to me, and I will send the manuscript to my friend Archibald Bell, the London bookseller.

Phillis (*with tears in her eyes*): Thank you again, sir. I am so grateful for all your support.

Susannah: We are grateful to you, Phillis. You have enriched our lives so much, and your poetry will continue to enrich and influence the lives of many generations to come in our young and promising land.

Narrator 1: John Wheatley sends Phillis's manuscript to England. Archibald Bell shows the poems to the countess of Huntingdon and she is very pleased with them. She asks if Phillis is a real person. The countess also is pleased that the book is dedicated to her. She requests that a picture of Phillis be engraved as the frontispiece of the book. Phillis has her friend and fellow slave Scipio Moorhead paint a portrait of her, and it is sent to London to be engraved.

Phillis travels to London for a change of climate to help her health and also to be there in person the day the volume comes off the press. She makes many friends in England, including Benjamin Franklin, who is quite impressed with her.

Phillis's book is a great success in America and England, and she continues to write more poems. She even writes one to George Washington, who, in return, invites her to visit him. By the time of her death in 1784, at the age of about 31, Phillis has written more than 70 poems about freedom, God, and being an enslaved person in the midst of a revolution.

Phillis Wheatley

Born around 1753 in the region of Senegal-Gambia, West Africa, Phillis Wheatley was stolen from her native land and taken to Boston, Massachusetts. She was sold to John and Susannah Wheatley, who named her after the vessel that had brought her to America.

Taught to read and write at a young age, Wheatley mastered English, Latin, and Greek. When her poems, which were laced with patriotic themes, began appearing in newspapers around Massachusetts, whites were unwilling to accept the fact that a slave girl had written them. In the early 1770s, Wheatley had to take a test to prove that she had actually written the poems bearing her name. Even though she passed the test, she was unable to find a Boston publisher and traveled to London, England.

In 1773, her collection *Poems on Various Subjects, Religious and Moral* was published. Soon after, she returned to the United States, and the Wheatleys freed her. Although she was criticized for allegedly ignoring the plight of black Americans, John Shields, editor of *The Collected Works of Phillis Wheatley*, maintains that a letter by Wheatley written after her emancipation proves that she was concerned "for the fate of her Black brothers and sisters still suffering under slavery."

In 1778, Wheatley married John Peters. She lived in poverty the rest of her life, and died at the birth of her third child on December 5, 1784.

Library of Congress

On Virtue

O Thou bright jewel in my aim I strive
To comprehend thee. Thine own words declare
Wisdom is higher than a fool can reach.
I cease to wonder, and no more attempt
Thine height t'explore, or fathom thy profound.
But, O my soul, sink not into despair,
Virtue is near thee, and with gentle hand
Would now embrace thee, hovers o'er
    thine head. . . .

—*Phillis Wheatley*

At Plimoth Plantation, 1627

© Fotolia/HIP

I magine if you could see, smell, hear, and feel the life of 17th-century Colonial New England, while interacting with the people who lived there. You might see a colonial joiner preparing wood to make chairs for use in village houses or smell seafood roasting over a fire outside of a traditional Native longhouse. You might hear a Pilgrim wife pounding corn for pudding or feel a finger-woven storage basket made by a Wampanoag woman. Imagine you could be face to face with history.

The English Pilgrim and Native Wampanoag history and way of life are preserved at Plimoth Plantation, a living history museum in Plymouth, Massachusetts. Visitors can walk through the colonial and Native homes, stores, workshops, and farmland, and speak with the role-players who recreate the lives of many of Plimoth Colony's original inhabitants. These roleplayers (or interpreters) speak using early modern English dialects (similar to those of Shakespeare) or a mix of English and Wampanoag languages, they share the unique viewpoints of the time period, and they demonstrate the common daily life of the times.

Meet Mistress Fuller, one Pilgrim wife, and read about her experiences, both before and during her life at Plimoth Plantation.

Plimoth Plantation

By 1627, the Pilgrims had built a thriving village of small homes and gardens. It is re-created at Plimoth Plantation. Gardens of fresh vegetables provided "sallets" for the Pilgrims' meals.

Why did you come to America?
My family has left England for matters of faith. In truth, we feel the king's church is somewhat corrupted and not as close to Scripture as it might be. Yet, to separate yourself out of the king's church 'tis to be counted an act of treason, and we were harried out of the land and so did dwell for many years in Holland.

But it grew very difficult even in Holland, for we lived as men in exile and in a very poor condition. The chiefest men of our congregation did look to settling in the New World, where we might raise our children English and in a true reformed church.

What did you think you would find here?
We knew not, certainly, what we should find in this wilderness. Some feared that, in truth, the changes of the air and the diet here should infect our bodies. And also we feared we should be in continual danger of the natural people here. But we put our trust in God, and he hath proved most merciful to us.

From the hilltop, you look down the sandy road lined on each side with sturdy little houses of weathered wood. In the distance, the ocean is deep green. Smoke from morning fires curls over the rooftops. Though the hour is early, the home of Mistress Fuller is already busy. Her husband, Samuel, is off to tend his fields, and she has finished milking her goats. She must weed her kitchen garden and pound Indian corn so she can make a pudding.

The Fullers' cottage has one room with clay daub walls. Some of their furniture has been made here, but other pieces, such as her husband's chair and a cupboard and chest, were brought from England. Mistress Fuller has lived in Plimoth for four years. Her husband came to the New World aboard the *Mayflower*—"a First Comer," she calls him—and she followed three years later.

How is your life at Plimoth different from your life in England or Holland?
For myself, I had always dwelt in cities, and here we are in the country, certain! In Holland, I spent most of my day spinning and then should go marketing for many of the things that I need. Here 'tis that I will do all for myself. I think none of us has ever had to pound corn ourselves, for it should always be brought to a mill.

There are times when the men will fetch in a deer that we might have venison to our table. Such a thing as that would be counted a luxury for a richer man at home in England.

It did take me some time to grow accustomed to how quiet it is here, where there are not markets and there are not people preaching and selling things in the street.

But it is a good place to raise my son here. He is born here and strong and healthful.

And he will be raised in a good reformed church, so I think any difficulties we have passed along the way have been to this end.

What are the villagers' feelings toward the Indians?

I think we have good treated peace with Massasoit's people and good trade with many of the other nations of Indians here. I do not find in these years that I grow fearful of the naturals. But Captain Standish keeps all our men well drilled. Our palisade about the village keeps us protected, and our fort is good and strong. Perhaps it is this sign that we are in great strength that does as well keep us safe here.

Certainly it is God's providence that the first naturals to come amongst us spoke English. They were as God's instruments here in the wilderness to help our way.

What types of foods do you prepare most often?

It depends upon the season. It is fish that is the chiefest meat on our tables in the summer months, and salads from our garden. And white meats, and by that I mean things made of milk and eggs. In the autumn and the winter months, the chiefest flesh is the pork that we have from our own hogs that we slaughter. There is also the great abundance of wildfowl in this place.

As far as sweetmeats, that is rare enough, for sugar is most costly. This spring my husband did purchase some sugar, but I will have to use it slowly and carefully, for I know not when I shall get some more. There are not honey bees here, so we have not the honey we had from the English country.

What I grow in my kitchen garden is just things to dress the pot and for salads, as well as herbs for medicines. Salad herbs are such as spinach and lettuce, and roots such as carrot.

The chiefest of the new foods that we have found here is the Indian corn. It is very coarse corn, more like oats in England. My husband prefers that I should cook it in puddings rather than to make bread of it, and then it is a good enough dish.

How do you make your family's clothes? What types of clothes do you wear?

I do not make all of the clothing for my family. I will make the shirts and smocks and aprons and caps. But mostly our suits, my husband's doublet and breeches, and my own waistcoat and petticoats are such as we have brought with us upon our coming or have been sent out of England made by tailors there. The cloth for the linens that I make must also come out of England.

For myself, it is underneath everything I wear a smock, which also serves as my night wear, and it is very similar to

In colonial times, the English often referred to Indians as "the naturals."

Preparing a meal for her family, Mistress Fuller slices pumpkins that she grew in her garden at Plimoth Plantation.

Plimoth Plantation

my husband's shirt, which he wears under everything. It is always of linen. And then over that, I shall set my bodices, and then a good many petticoats of woolen cloth, and then a waistcoat I will wear over that, and about my waist my apron and my girdle. Upon my head I wear a coif of linen. In the winter, I have a cloak to set about me and some mittens I have knit and a muffler to put about my chin. And hose, of course, and our leather shoeing. My husband over his shirt has his doublet and his breeches to wear and similar warmer things as myself to wear in the winter.

Herbs were grown for medicinal purposes.

How do you educate your children at Plimoth?

There is not a school here. My father did teach me to read so that I might read Scripture, and so my son will be taught, as well as any daughters that I have. You will find some of the folk, especially those who are not of our church, perhaps do not value reading so highly for their daughters. But before even our children are taught to read, they must be taught to make their way in the world. So lads, when they are six or seven years old, go about with their father to learn his trade. And lasses, of the same age, will be learning to help their mothers so that they might themselves keep a house.

What do you do for leisure? How much leisure time do you have?

'Tis to my mind a somewhat curious question, for we are not gentlefolk here. It is gentlemen and gentlewomen who do not have to labor for their livings. But for myself, there is always a labor to look to except upon the Sabbath. It does not mean I do not amuse myself, for my son does bring me great joy. And sometimes I will set to doing some chore with my sister. Then we have time to recount stories or to sing and talk with one another, and I find that pleasurable. I do also enjoy to hear my husband read out of the Scriptures to me.

There are different occasions out of the ordinary that bring joy. Well . . . shortly after I arrived here, Master Bradford did take for his wife Mistress Alice, and their wedding was quite a grand thing, even with King Massasoit and many Indians coming to it.

What are some of your common medicines, and how do you make them?

In the garden, I do grow all manner of herbs that I might use to keep my family in good health. I do grow lilies what I will take the flower and pound of it, and set it in the oil of olives sunning in a glass. 'Tis very good for rubbing to the temples for a headache, and 'tis also good in my duties as a midwife. I have some skill at midwifery, and many of the women will look to me for help at that time. Other medicines are simply made by boiling a bit of the leaf, or it might be the flower, or it might be the root of a plant, and drinking it down. Some of the herbs dry very well so that you might use them the whole year round.

My husband hath some skill at surgery, so if someone needs a tooth pulled or blood let, or an ulcer lanced, he hath the tools for that.

If you could look into the future and invent something to make life easier, what would you do?

There again is a question I find curious and doth bring a smile to my lips, for I think looking into the future, it is known only to God. Certainly I hope it is in God's plan that my son should grow strong and to come into his own land. I look to someday soon have a good, learned man sent amongst us as a pastor in our church. And I think, like all housewives in New Plimoth, I look to the time we have a mill here that our corn might be ground and not pounded ourselves. But all these things I leave to God's will.

WETAMO
INDIAN QUEEN

At a time in American history when most women did not have a lot of power, there was one woman who became a sachem, or queen, of the Wampanoag Native American tribe. Her name was Wetamo, and during the conflict called King Philip's War (1675-1676), she became a respected leader of her people. She was one of the most powerful Native American women in colonial times.

It is believed that Wetamo was born in the early 1630's. In 1620, the Wampanoag chief Massasoit befriended the English colonists when they settled at Plymouth, ensuring their survival in the new world. Edward Winslow and other early leaders developed a mutual respect with Massasoit and the Wampanoag. In 1621, the Wampanoag and colonists signed a treaty of peace which lasted for more than 50 years, throughout Massasoit's

lifetime. As more and more English arrived to settle the colonies, however, life began to change for Wetamo and her people. It is reported that between 1630 and 1640, 20,000 English colonists came to New England.

Wetamo's first husband, Wamsutta, was the son of the Wampanoag leader Massasoit. Massasoit asked that his two sons, Wamsutta and Metacomet, be given English names, Alexander and Philip. Wamsutta (Alexander) was the older brother of Metacomet (Philip), who was married to Wetamo's sister. When Massasoit died in 1661, Wamsutta became the sachem of the tribe. But soon there were

Wetamo swimming in the Matapoisett River to escape from colonial soldiers during King Philip's War.

conflicts with the English settlers. They wanted more and more tribal lands. Wamsutta was arrested by the English and died mysteriously while he was jailed. Now Metacomet, or Philip, became the leader or "king" of his people. Wetamo became sachem, hence the name Queen Wetamo, of her town, Pocasset, in what is now Rhode Island. She was the ruler of 300 warriors. In 1665, the Wampanoag chiefs informed settlers that they were to stay off the Native American lands. Metacomet tried unsuccessfully to unite the Indian peoples to prevent the English settlers from encroaching even more on their lands. For ten years Wetamo helped her brother-in-law Metacomet (Philip) as he tried to maintain a good relationship with the settlers.

When Metacomet stopped trying to keep the peace with the American colonists and decide to fight them, Wetamo decided to support him. This led to King Philip's War, as the tribes began to fight

Metacomet (King Philip)

Indian History for Young Folks, by Francis S. Drake, 1884

back by killing settlers and destroying their towns. Her loyalty was to her own people. She was already an enemy of the English because she had lands that they wanted. She no longer wanted to give up her tribal lands as well as the ability of her people to govern themselves. When her second husband said that he would still be loyal to the English, Wetamo left him to join Metacomet's warriors. She would marry a third time, to Quanopin, a sachem of the Narragansett tribe. Quanopin, Wetamo, and Metacomet traveled together, fighting the English but also fleeing from the colonial soldiers.

At this time, a woman named Mary Rowlandson had been captured by the Wampanoag when they raided Lancaster, Massachusetts. She was forced to live with them for more than eleven weeks. Years later Mary wrote a book about her experiences as a captive of the Wampanoag. She described the powerful sachem:

> *A severe and proud dame she was, bestowing every day in dressing herself neat as much time as any of the gentry of the land: powdering her hair, and painting her face, going with necklaces, with jewels in her ears, and bracelets upon her hands.*

The raid on Lancaster was one of the last successful battles for Metacomet and his warriors. Soon after, Quanopin was captured and shot. Wetamo's sister and her young son were captured and sold as slaves.

Wetamo and the rest of her warriors continued to run from the colonial soldiers, but when they tried to return home to Pocasset, they were ambushed. Everyone except Wetamo was apparently killed or captured, as she was not found among the victims. No one knew what had happened to her, although some versions of the story say she had escaped and tried to cross a river. A group of settlers later found the body of a Native American woman who had apparently drowned in a river. She was beheaded and her head was displayed on a pole in the town of Taunton as a warning to other tribe members. But no one was sure if it was Wetamo. Increase Mather, a colonial minister and writer, described how the

Indian prisoners realized it was their Wampanoag queen. "The Indians who were prisoners there, knew it presently, and made a most horrible and diabolical Lamentation, crying out that it was their Queen's head." Metacomet was killed soon after. His head was also placed on a pole next to Wetamo's. King Philip's War was soon over.

Between 1675 and 1676, six hundred colonists lost their lives in King Philip's War. Three thousand Native Americans died. Out of ninety English villages, fifty were attacked by the Indians. Even peaceful tribes, such as the Narragansett, who did not for the most part join in the war, were victims, killed because the settlers feared all Indians and attacked where they could. Many innocent people—both English settlers and Native Americans—died in these violent conflicts.

Like the other members of the Wampanoag and Narragansett tribes, Wetamo was fighting to keep the territories that had been her people's for many, many years before the English ever came to America. Although Wetamo and her people were nearly wiped out, some did survive, living with other tribes or escaping to live in other parts of New England, where their descendants still live today. But Wetamo, queen of her people, was a true leader at a time when most women had almost no power at all.

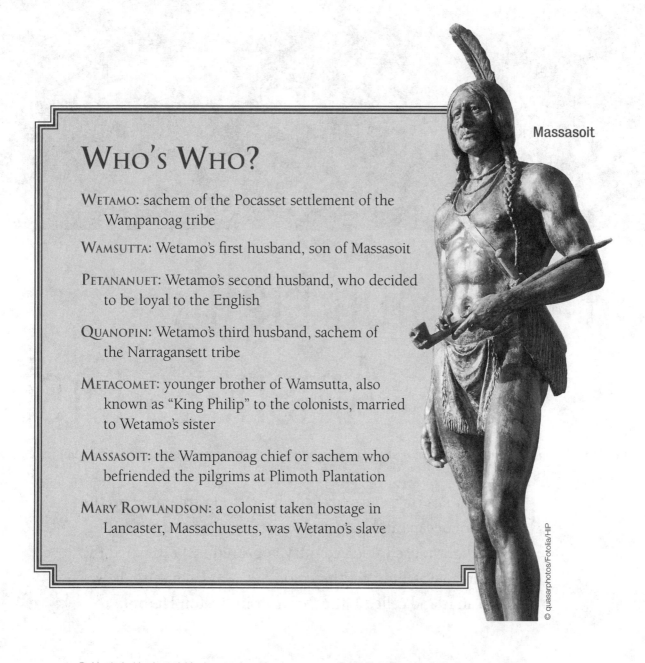

Massasoit

WHO'S WHO?

WETAMO: sachem of the Pocasset settlement of the Wampanoag tribe

WAMSUTTA: Wetamo's first husband, son of Massasoit

PETANANUET: Wetamo's second husband, who decided to be loyal to the English

QUANOPIN: Wetamo's third husband, sachem of the Narragansett tribe

METACOMET: younger brother of Wamsutta, also known as "King Philip" to the colonists, married to Wetamo's sister

MASSASOIT: the Wampanoag chief or sachem who befriended the pilgrims at Plimoth Plantation

MARY ROWLANDSON: a colonist taken hostage in Lancaster, Massachusetts, was Wetamo's slave

© quasarphotos/Fotolia/HIP

By Marcia Amidon Lusted. May be reproduced for classroom use. *Toolkit Texts: Short Nonfiction for American History, Colonial Times* by Stephanie Harvey and Anne Goudvis, ©2014 (Portsmouth, NH: Heinemann).

Boston Lighthouse, Boston, Massachusetts, USA © Ocean/Corbis

The Boston Light:
America's First

Lighthouses of various kinds have stood solemnly on the shores of oceans and waterways ever since man began sailing. The first lighthouse in our country appeared in 1716 when the Boston light was built by the colony of Massachusetts. It was built on an island called Little Brewster in Boston Harbor.

Before that, only bonfires or blazing barrels of pitch, maintained by shipowners and merchants along high points of the coast near cities, guided ships to port. During the day a smoldering fire that produced a pillar of smoke was used. At night, the ships were guided by a briskly burning fire. As soon as an approaching ship was sighted, the fire was lit to help guide the ship into the harbor.

Unfortunately, unscrupulous persons would sometimes build a fire or signal in a dangerous place to purposely lure a ship onto the rocks. The people who did this were called "moon cussers," taking their name from the fact that they prayed for moonless nights when ships might run aground. "Moon cussers" built their shore fires on bluffs by the most dangerous reefs and rocks. The ship captains would sail towards the light thinking it was the entrance to the harbor and realize too late that they had been deceived. The ship's cargo of silks, spices, and other treasures would be looted as it washed up on the shores.

Finally, the merchants of Boston took action against these thieves and presented a petition to the General Court in 1713. Three years later, on September 14, 1716, the light was lit in America's first lighthouse.

This first lighthouse, a cone-shaped tower built of stone, stood 60 feet high. It was painted white so that it could be easily recognized. An iron cage at the

||||||||||||||||||||||||||||||||||||||||||||||||||

The Boston lighthouse, built in 1716 on Little Brewster Island in Boston Harbor, was the first lighthouse to appear in our country.

||||||||||||||||||||||||||||||||||||||||||||||||||

top was covered by a copper roof that was supported by a brick arch. Inside the cage were very crude lanterns with heavy wooden frames holding small, thick panes of glass.

The Boston light was first lit by tallow candles, but these were quickly replaced by oil lamps with wicks that burned fish oil or whale oil. This fuel produced a great deal of black sooty smoke that frequently had to be cleaned off the glass panes. The lamps had to be refilled with oil two or three times a night.

The first keeper of the light, George Worthylake, met a tragic death two years after he took the post. He, his wife, and their daughter drowned when the lighthouse boat capsized in a storm.

Benjamin Franklin was 13 years old at the time. He heard of the incident and wrote a ballad called "Lighthouse Tragedy" which he sold on the streets of Boston for a penny a copy.

In 1719, the new keeper, John Hayes, began using what was to be America's first "fog signal." He pulled a cannon up on the grounds below the lighthouse and fired it at regular intervals whenever fog kept the Boston light from being seen. All seagoing vessels at this time carried cannons aboard for protection against pirates. As a shipmaster approached Boston Harbor, he would fire his cannon and wait for the reply from the lighthouse cannon that would tell him approximately his position in the harbor. Unfortunately, the wind often carried the sound of the cannon in the wrong direction.

Boston Lighthouse, Boston, Massachusetts, USA © Ocean/Corbis

IIIIIIIIIIIIIIIIIIIIIIIIIIIIIIIIIIIIIIIIIII

FOR THE NEXT FORTY YEARS the Boston light peacefully served its purpose, but as our colonial government moved closer to war with Britain, trouble began.

Boston Harbor was important to the economy of both the colonies and the British Empire. A seesaw battle for ownership of the lighthouse began. Whoever could capture the lighthouse could then control the harbor. Finally, after a battle with the colonists under the leadership of General Washington, the British pulled their ships out of the harbor— but not before a time charge had been set to blow up the lighthouse.

The Boston light was destroyed, but the colonists were able to save the metal top, which was melted down and made into cannon ladles. The ladles were long-handled spoons used to load gunpowder into cannons during the Revolutionary War.

From June of 1776 to 1783, the harbor light was abandoned. Then, in 1783, the Massachusetts legislature provided money for a new Boston light to be built on the site of the old lighthouse. The new Boston light was 75 feet high, including the lantern, but was raised to a height of 89 feet in 1859. That structure is standing today, and serves as a monument to America's first lighthouse.

By Dianne MacMillan, *Cobblestone*, © by Carus Publishing Company. Reproduced with permission.
May be reproduced for classroom use. *Toolkit Texts: Short Nonfiction for American History, Colonial Times*
by Stephanie Harvey and Anne Goudvis, ©2014 (Portsmouth, NH: Heinemann).

"Combine ourselves into a civil Body Politick"

THE MAYFLOWER COMPACT

In the name of God Amen. We whose names are underwritten, the loyall subjects of our dread sovereign Lord King James by the grace of God, of great Britaine, Franc, & Ireland kind, defender of the faith, & c.

Having undertaken for the Glory of God, and Advancement of the Christian Faith, and the Honour of our King and Country, a voyage to plant the first colony in the northern Parts of Virginia; do by these Presents, solemnly and mutually in the Presence of God and one another, covenant and combine ourselves together into a civil Body Politick, for our better Ordering and Preservation, and Furtherance of the Ends aforesaid; And by Virtue hereof to enact, constitute, and frame, such just and equal Laws, Ordinances, Acts, Constitutions and Offices, from time to time, as shall be thought most meet and convenient for the General good of the Colony; unto which we promise all due Submission and Obedience.

In witnes whereof we have hereunder subscribed our names at Cap-Codd the 11 of November, in the year of the raigne of our soveraigne Lord King James of England, France, & Ireland the eighteenth and of Scotland the fiftie fourth. An: Com. 1620

Of Plymouth Plantation

WILLIAM BRADFORD

Of Plymouth Plantation is the journal of William Bradford, the leader of the Plymouth Colony in Massachusetts. The journal describes the story of the Pilgrims from 1608 when they settled in the Dutch Republic through the voyage of the *Mayflower* in 1620 and the early years of the Colony they founded until 1647. The book ends with a list of the *Mayflower* passengers and what happened to them.

About the voyage to the New World:

After they had enjoyed fair winds and weather for a season, they were encountered many times with cross winds, and met with many fierce storms, with which the ship was shrewdly shaken, and her upper works made very leaky; and one of the main beams in the mid ships was bowed and cracked, which put them in some fear that the ship could not be able to perform the voyage. . . . But in examining of all opinions, the master and others affirmed they knew the ship to be strong and firm under water; and for the buckling of the main beam, there was a great iron screw the passengers brought out of Holland, which would raise the beam into place; the which being done, the carpenter and the master affirmed that with a post put under it, set firm in the lower deck, and otherways bound, he would make it sufficient. And as for the decks and upper works they would caulk them as well as they could, and thought with the working of the ship they would not long keep staunch [watertight] yet there would otherwise be no great danger, if they did not overpress her with sails. So they committed themselves to the will of God, and resolved to proceed . . .

Arriving after their long ocean journey:

. . . after long beating at sea they fell with that land which is called Cape Cod; the which being made and certainly known to be it, they were not a little joyful. After some deliberation had amongst themselves and with the master of the ship, they tacked about and resolved to stand for the southward (the wind and weather being fair) to find some place about Hudson's River for their habitation. But after they sailed the course about half the day, they fell amongst dangerous shoals and roaring breakers, and they were so far entangled therewith as they conceived themselves in great danger; and the wind shrinking upon them withal, they resolved to bear up again for the Cape, and thought themselves happy to get out of those dangers before night overtook them, as by God's providence they did. And the next day they got into the Cape-harbor where they rid in safety . . .

Being thus arrived in good harbor and brought safe to land, they fell upon their knees and blessed the God of heaven, who had brought them over the vast and furious ocean, and delivered them from all the perils and miseries thereof, again to set their feet on the firm and stable earth, their proper element.

. . . they had now no friends to welcome them, nor inns to entertain or refresh their weather-beaten bodies, no houses or much less towns to repair to, to seek for succor. . . . And for the season it was winter, and they that know the winters of that country know them to be sharp and violent, and subject to cruel and fierce storms, dangerous to travel to known places, much more to search an unknown coast. Besides, what could they see but a hideous and desolate wilderness, full of wild beasts and wild men? And what multitudes there might be of them they knew not.

Starving Time

In these hard and difficult beginnings they found some discontents and murmurings arise amongst some, and mutinous speeches and carriages in others; but they were soon quelled and overcome by the wisdom, patience, and just and equal carriage of things by the Governor [John Carver] and better part, which clove faithfully together in the main. But that which was most sad and lamentable was, that in 2 or 3 months' time half of their company died, especially in January: and February, being the depth of winter, and wanting houses and other comforts; being infected with the scurvy and other diseases, which this long voyage and their inaccomodate condition had brought upon them; so as there died some times 2 or 3 of a day, in the foresaid time; that of 100 and odd persons, scarce 50 remained. And of these in the time of most distress, there was but 6 or 7 persons, who, to their great commendations be it spoke, spared no pains, night nor day, but with abundance of toil and hazard of their own health, fetched them wood, made them fires, dressed them meat, made their beds, washed their loathsome clothes, clothed and unclothed them; in a word, did all the homely and necessary offices for them which dainty and queasy stomachs cannot endure to hear named; and all this willingly and cheerfully, without any grudging in the least, showing herein their true love unto their friends and brethren. A rare example and worthy to be remembered. Two of these 7 were Mr. William Brewster, their reverend Elder, and Myles Standish, their Captain and military commander, unto whom myself and many others, were much beholden on our low and sick condition.

Indian Relations

All this while the Indians came skulking about them, and would sometimes show themselves aloof off, but when any approached near them, they would run away. And once they stole away their tools where they had been at work, and were gone to dinner. But about the 16th of March a certain Indian came boldly amongst them, and spoke to them in broken English, which they could well understand, but marveled at it. At length they understood by discourse with him, that he was not of these parts, but belonged to the eastern parts, where some English ships came to fish, with whom he was acquainted, and could name sundry of them by their names, amongst whom he had got his language. He became profitable to them in acquainting them with many things concerning the state of the country in the east parts where he lived, which was afterwards profitable unto them; as also of the people here, of their names, number, and strength; of their situation and distance from this place, and who was chief amongst them. His name was Samaset; he told them also of another Indian whose name was Squanto, a native of this place, who had been in England and could speak better English than himself. Being, after some time of entertainment and gifts, dismissed, a while after he came again, and 5 more with him, and they brought again all the tools that were stolen away before, and made way for the coming of their great Sachem, called Massasoyt; who, about 4 or 5 days after, came with the chief of his friends and other attendance, with the aforesaid Squanto. With whom, after friendly entertainment, and some gifts given him, they made peace with him (which hath now continued this 24 years) in these terms:

1. That neither he nor any of his should injure or do hurt to any of their people.

2. That if any of his did any hurt to any of theirs, he would send the offender, that they might punish him.

3. That if anything were taken away from any of theirs, he should cause it to be restored; and they should do the like to his.

4. If any did unjustly war against him, they would aid him; if any did war against them, he should aid them.

5. He should send to his neighbors confederates, to certify them of this, that they might not wrong them, but might be likewise comprised in the conditions of peace.

6. That when their men came to them, they should leave their bows and arrows behind them.

After these things he returned to his place called Sowams, some 40 miles from this place, but Squanto continued with them, and was their interpreter, and was a special instrument sent of God for their good beyond their expectation. He directed them how to set their corn, where to take fish, and to procure other commodities, and was also their pilot to bring them to unknown places for their profit, and never left them till he died.

Ben Franklin's CITY

C olonial Philadelphia could be considered almost as much the creation of Benjamin Franklin as it was of William Penn. It is true that when Franklin opened his printing shop in Philadelphia in 1728, this important city already was forty-six years old. But it also was a city without organized firefighters, an effective police force, or a hospital. These and other improvements would be Franklin's contributions.

Even before opening his printing shop, Franklin had formed a club in Philadelphia called the *Junto*. Devoted to self-improvement and community service, its members helped Franklin bring about many important changes in the city over time.

Books and paper were valuable things in colonial times, making Franklin's circulating library (top) a remarkable addition to the city. The man himself (left), painted by Charles Willson Peale.

The First Library

The Junto's first project was to create a library. Since books were expensive and Philadelphia had no public libraries, Franklin suggested that the Junto form its own library by having each member contribute books to a common supply. This worked so well that Franklin decided to form a subscription library, which anyone could join by paying an annual fee. The fees collected paid for the purchase of books as well as a librarian. This became known as America's first

A **junto** is a small, usually secret, group united for a common interest.

By Jerry Miller, *Cobblestone*, © by Carus Publishing Company. Reproduced with permission. May be reproduced for classroom use. *Toolkit Texts: Short Nonfiction for American History, Colonial Times* by Stephanie Harvey and Anne Goudvis, ©2014 (Portsmouth, NH: Heinemann).

The Library Company of Pennsylvania

Pennsylvania Hospital was yet another endeavor supported by Franklin.

A **circulating library**, also known as a lending library, allows books to be checked out for a certain period of time.

Riffraff are people regarded as worthless.

circulating library. In a way, it also could be considered America's first free public library, since even nonmembers could use the books if they read them inside the building.

Fire and Public Safety

Franklin's next project was to improve the city's firefighting services. The volunteers who fought Philadelphia's fires often had no equipment. They also had little knowledge of the best ways to save homes, businesses, and other buildings from destruction.

Franklin believed that well-organized volunteer "companies" should be formed. They could raise money for equipment, train their members, and fight all the fires within their districts—Franklin started the first fire company himself. Others soon followed. Franklin later wrote that he believed there was no city in the world where fires were put out more quickly than in Philadelphia.

With the city safer from fire, Franklin tackled crime. Philadelphia had a police system—of sorts. Constables were appointed to protect their areas of the city, and property owners were supposed to help by taking turns patrolling the streets at night. However, most citizens

paid to have substitutes take their place. Constables would use a small part of this money to hire **riffraff** as patrolmen and keep the rest for themselves. All too often, the substitutes spent their time drinking in taverns instead of patrolling. Franklin proposed to raise money through a property tax to pay for respectable, full-time police officers. For many years, Philadelphia's political leaders opposed this plan, but it was finally adopted in 1752.

Scientific and Intellectual Societies

Franklin next established America's first scientific society. As a writer and publisher of newspapers, books, and magazines, he had done his best to keep Philadelphians well informed. When he became Philadelphia's postmaster, Franklin's reforms made communication with other colonies easier, cheaper, and faster. (Franklin eventually became head of the postal service for all the colonies.) But Franklin wanted to do something to keep colonial scientists up-to-date with new ideas and discoveries. So, he started the American Philosophical Society. Since Philadelphia was its headquarters, that city benefited most from its formation.

But even with an organization for the advancement of science, the Colonies still had only four colleges—Harvard, Princeton, William and Mary, and Yale. And none of them was in Pennsylvania. In 1749, Franklin wrote a pamphlet describing the college he felt Pennsylvania should establish. This resulted in widespread support for the idea. The Academy and College of Philadelphia—now the University of Pennsylvania—was founded in 1751.

The First Hospital

Thomas Bond provided Franklin with his next project. Bond was a physician who wanted to build a hospital like those he had seen in Europe. He had no luck gaining support for his plan until he went to Franklin, who liked the idea and agreed to take charge of fundraising. Franklin was so successful that nearly every wealthy or middle-class Philadelphian contributed to the building of America's first hospital. The Pennsylvania Hospital soon became world-famous, especially for its treatment of the mentally ill.

A Clean, Bright, Safe City

Another problem Philadelphia faced was its unpaved streets. In wet weather, the roads were muddy; in dry weather, dust blew everywhere. Franklin campaigned for the paving of Philadelphia's streets, then organized a merchant's association to fund their sweeping. He also joined another campaign aimed at lighting the dark streets at night. Franklin even invented a lamp that made the city brighter than London. Dark, dirty, muddy Philadelphia became clean, bright, and safe.

All of this progress took place between 1730 and 1757 and resulted in a city many believed was the second greatest (after London) in the British Empire. Not all of these improvements began with Franklin, and each one became possible only through the hard work and financial support of many. Nevertheless, it is still tempting to call the Philadelphia of the mid-1700s "Ben Franklin's City."

Franklin's practical ideas greatly improved the city—he organized a firefighting corps (below) and supported a school for higher learning. The Academy (left) eventually became today's University of Pennsylvania.

Franklin helped form The Philadelphia Contributionship, a fire insurance company. The symbol (above) displayed on a house indicated that the owner had purchased a policy from the company.

Courtesy of The Philadelphia Contributionship

Indian History for Young Folks by Francis S. Drake, 1884

*B*orn in Boston in 1706, **Benjamin Franklin** was a city dweller his whole life. Although he lived in London and Paris at times, the bustling city of Philadelphia was his home for most of his life. In Philadelphia, Franklin became a fine printer, a clever writer, a great thinker, and a good citizen.

1706 Born January 17, the ninth of eleven children born to Josiah and Abiah Franklin

1716 Works in his father's candle-making shop

1718 Begins an apprenticeship in his brother's printing shop in Boston

1723 Runs away to Philadelphia and works in the printing shop

1724 Sails for England on November 5, continuing his training as a printer

1726 Returns to Philadelphia and works as clerk, bookkeeper, and shopkeeper

1727 Forms the Junto, a club for "self-improvement, study, mutual aid, and conviviality"

1728 Co-founds a printing shop

1729 Purchases The Pennsylvania Gazette, which becomes renowned for its strong influence on public opinion

1731 Establishes The Library Company of Philadelphia, the first lending library in America

Issues the first edition of Poor Richard's Almanack, an instant best-seller that quickly becomes the most popular almanac in the colonies

1736 Helps found the Union Fire Company, which organizes and trains teams of firemen

1737 Begins service as postmaster of Philadelphia, continuing until 1753

1749 Founds the Academy and College of Philadelphia, later renamed the University of Pennsylvania

1751 Co-founds the Pennsylvania Hospital, the colonies' first public hospital

1752 Performs kite and key experiment, confirming his theory that electricity existed in thunderclouds in the form of lightning

1757 Appointed colonial agent to London. Lives and works in London for the next eighteen years

1775 Arrives back in Philadelphia

Elected the Pennsylvania delegate to the Second Continental Congress

1776 Serves on the committee to draft the Declaration of Independence

Appointed commissioner to the court of France

1783 Helps negotiate and signs Treaty of Paris, officially ending the Revolutionary War

1785 Moves back to Philadelphia

1787 Elected president of the Pennsylvania Society for Promoting the Abolition of Slavery

Serves as delegate to the Constitutional Convention

1790 Dies on April 17, 1790, at the age of eighty-four

Poor Richard, 1733.

AN

Almanack

For the Year of Chrift

1 7 3 3,

Being the Firft after LEAP YEAR:

And makes fince the Creation	Years
By the Account of the Eaftern *Greeks*	7241
By the Latin Church, when ☉ ent. ♈	6932
By the Computation of *W. W.*	5742
By the *Roman* Chronology	5682
By the *Jewish* Rabbies	5494

Wherein is contained

The Lunations, Eclipfes, Judgment of the Weather, Spring Tides, Planets Motions & mutual Afpects, Sun and Moon's Rifing and Setting, Length of Days, Time of High Water, Fairs, Courts, and obfervable Days.

Fitted to the Latitude of Forty Degrees, and a Meridian of Five Hours Weft from *London*, but may without fenfible Error, ferve all the adjacent Places, even from *Newfoundland* to *South-Carolina.*

By *RICHARD SAUNDERS*, Philom.

PHILADELPHIA:
Printed and fold by *B. FRANKLIN*, at the New Printing-Office near the Market.

Library of Congress

Library of Congress

BUTCHERS, BAKERS, and BONNETMAKERS

Rebecca Jones was a **spinster**. A Quaker minister since she was nineteen, Jones shared a Philadelphia home with her friend, Hannah Catherall. In 1763, they opened a school together. The two women taught girls how to spell, read, and sew—typical lessons for females of that day. But Jones and Catherall also taught French, "arithmetick," and poetry, which were courses generally reserved for boys.

If Jones had lived in any one of the other colonies during this time, her life would probably have been different. Most colonial customs dictated that marriage and motherhood were the primary purposes in a woman's life. But Philadelphia was unique. As a city based on tolerance, it offered a home to women of many backgrounds.

The citizens of Philadelphia were more accepting of less traditional values. While many colonists read only the Bible, Philadelphians had access to literature from all over the world because a variety of books and magazines arrived at their port city. These opened their minds to women who were not the typical wives and mothers of colonial days.

The influence of Quaker beliefs also broadened views of womanhood in Philadelphia. Quakers felt that men and women were equal in the eyes of God. They encouraged women to become ministers and to speak

A **spinster** is a woman who never marries.

JONES & CATHERALL SCHOOL ESTABLISHED 1763

Midwifery is the profession of assisting women during childbirth.

Housewifery is the role of a married woman who manages a home.

Mantuas were loose-fitting gowns worn by women in the 17th and 18th centuries.

A **tallow chandler** is one who makes or sells candles.

out in public and participate in politics. (In most colonies, only men enjoyed those activities.) Quakers also believed that women need not marry and have children in order to have successful lives and be respectable members of society.

But there was no getting around housework. Women spent many hours each day cooking, cleaning, sewing, and taking care of their households. And in Colonial Philadelphia, households often included caring for or overseeing apprentices, servants, and boarders.

Slave women particularly filled household jobs of cooking, cleaning, and caring for children.

Philadelphia women who worked outside the home usually practiced traditionally female occupations, such as **midwifery** and sewing. Young girls learned these trades through apprenticeships. When she was seven, Mary Denny joined the household of Ralph Collins to learn **housewifery**. Lydia Whitehead became an apprentice to a bonnet-, hat-, and cloakmaker. Elizabeth Fox apprenticed to learn how to make **mantuas**. Another girl was taught the "mystery" of baking gingerbread.

The women of Philadelphia often entered into business by working alongside their husbands. Deborah Franklin, Benjamin Franklin's wife, tracked accounts for the Franklins' dry goods shop. Other women took on commercial responsibilities when their husbands went off to sea.

Women who were widowed tended to continue their husbands' trades. Ann Wishart supported her family as a **tallow chandler** after her husband

By Heather M. Hopkins, illustrated by Margaret Lindmark, *Cobblestone*, © by Carus Publishing Company. Reproduced with permission. May be reproduced for classroom use. *Toolkit Texts: Short Nonfiction for American History, Colonial Times* by Stephanie Harvey and Anne Goudvis, ©2014 (Portsmouth, NH: Heinemann).

died. In 1773, Elizabeth Lawrence advertised in the *Pennsylvania Gazette* newspaper that she planned to carry on her late husband's upholstery business. Rachel Draper did well enough running a tavern by herself to send her two daughters to Jones and Catherall's school.

Historically, widows have felt pressure to remarry, but those living in Colonial Philadelphia often did not. Some went on to start their own businesses, like Hannah Breintnall, who opened the Hen and Chickens Tavern after her husband died.

Breintnall later ran an optician's shop, where she sold magnifying glasses, telescopes, and eyeglasses "of the finest Crystal."

One need only glance at the tax records of Colonial Philadelphia to see the range of choices available to that city's women. Most women were wives and mothers, but some also were butchers, bakers, **apothecaries**, grocers, innkeepers, booksellers, glovers, soapboilers, blacksmiths, tailors, **tinkers**, and leather breeches makers.

What would you be?

Apothecaries, or pharmacists, sell medicine.

Tinkers repair metal household utensils, like pots and pans.

LIFE IN Colonial Maryland

From Maryland's first settlement in 1634 until the 1770s, tobacco and corn were the most important crops. Corn was the main food in Colonial Maryland, and tobacco was sold in Europe in return for clothing, tools, and other manufactured materials. The planting, growing, and cultivating of tobacco and corn required a great deal of labor, though. A constant supply of unmarried **indentured** servants was needed to help work the fields. Working on tobacco crops in the hope of finding better opportunities brought many English, Scottish, and Irish immigrants to Maryland.

Hard Life in a New Land

Whether settlers were masters or servants, their lives were not easy. Between the backbreaking work in the fields and various diseases, many immigrants died young, usually before their children were of an age to inherit property. If children had lost both parents and had no surviving relatives, the courts assigned them to other families. Poor children were forced to pay for their room and board by becoming servants in these families until they were old enough to support themselves.

Yet for settlers who survived, Maryland's profitable tobacco economy offered opportunities even for those who came as servants. Servants had to pay for their passage across the ocean with four or five years of labor, but once they

Indentured means sold into the service of another for a specific amount of time.

By Lois Green Carr, illustrated by Mark Mitchell, *Cobblestone*, © by Carus Publishing Company. Reproduced with permission.
May be reproduced for classroom use. *Toolkit Texts: Short Nonfiction for American History, Colonial Times*
by Stephanie Harvey and Anne Goudvis, ©2014 (Portsmouth, NH: Heinemann).

were free, their masters owed them freedom dues: enough corn to feed them for a year and seed for the following year; clothing; and, for men, an axe and hoe. If a planter would lease a man some land and allow him to build a house on it, all a former servant needed to set up housekeeping was a bed to sleep on and a pot for cooking. After some years, profits from growing tobacco could pay for land of his own. Or he could work for wages until he had saved enough money to purchase land. Ex-servant women quickly married, since many fewer women than men made the journey from Great Britain.

Life Improves

The 1700s brought social changes that altered the character of Maryland. Immigration slowed down, partly because opportunities for work had improved back in England. Native-born settlers dominated the population of Maryland. With improved immunity against diseases, families increased in size, stability, and life expectancy. Fathers began to live long enough to pass on their estates and social positions to their sons.

Maryland's economy also changed in the 1700s. With virgin forests disappearing, the new growth was easier to clear, as were the forests' huge root systems. Plowing became possible, and planters added English grains, especially wheat, to their farms. New grain crops made tobacco less crucial for prosperity. Larger families meant time for home industries, such as **dairying**, **spinning**, and weaving, which improved family income.

> **Dairying** is the business of turning cow's milk into butter and cheese for sale.
>
> **Spinning** is the process of making material into yarn or thread.

Disparities Grow

There were negative changes, too. With a growing population, the availability of land to own became limited, and the price of good land increased. The opportunities of the 1600s for poor men to become landowners and move up in society declined.

Even more important was the shift from indentured servants to slave labor. Planters relied more and more on the use of enslaved Africans and their descendants. Slaveholding greatly increased the growing distance between poor planters and rich landowners in the Maryland society of the 1700s.

Until late in the 1600s, Maryland offered opportunities for people who came with nothing to acquire land and status. There was religious freedom for all Christians.

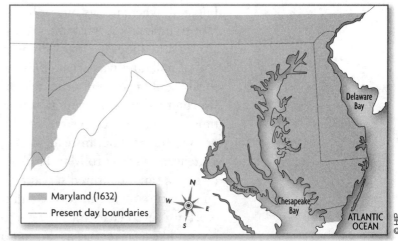

Maryland (1632)
.... Present day boundaries

COLONIAL MARYLAND

Molly Bannaky

I n 1683, an English ship sailed into the colony of Maryland in the new world of America. On board was a seventeen year old girl named Molly Walsh. She was being sent to the colonies because she had committed a crime. Molly was a dairymaid in a manor house in England, where it was one of her jobs to milk cows. According to the stories told about her, Molly stole a pail of milk and was arrested. Because Molly could read and write, which was unusual for a servant at that time, she did not receive the death penalty for stealing. Instead, she was sentenced to travel to Maryland and be sold as an indentured servant. As an indentured servant, Molly had to work for seven years for no wages, almost like a slave. But at the end of that time she would earn her freedom and be given a small piece of land for her own.

No one knows if the stories told about Molly and handed down through history are really true. But according to those stories, Molly stepped off the ship in Maryland after months at sea. She was sold to a man who owned a tobacco farm. She learned to plow and tend to tobacco plants. She also sewed, nursed the sick, and did many other chores as well. Finally, after seven years, she earned her freedom. Molly was given an ox, a cart, seeds and a plow, clothing, a gun, and a small parcel of land on Patapsco River near Baltimore, Maryland. In just one year, she built a cabin and planted corn and tobacco. She even earned

By Marcia Amidon Lusted. May be reproduced for classroom use. *Toolkit Texts: Short Nonfiction for American History,*
Colonial Times by Stephanie Harvey and Anne Goudvis, ©2014 (Portsmouth, NH: Heinemann).

enough money to buy two African slaves to help her on her farm.

One slave, whose name is not known, worked hard and helped Molly. The other slave, whose name was Bannka, told Molly that he was a prince, the son of a king back in Africa. According to a biography of Molly's grandson, Bannka was "a man of industry, integrity, fine disposition and dignified manners." Molly freed him from slavery, and soon after she married Bannka. He kept his African name, but Molly changed it to Bannaky as her new last name.

Molly and Bannka had four daughters together: Mary, Katherine, Esther and Jemima. Bannka died very young, leaving Molly to run her farm and raise her girls by herself. Molly's daughter Mary, when she grew up, also purchased an African slave and then married him. His American name was Robert and he also used Bannaky as a last name. Mary and Robert's oldest child, a son, was named Benjamin. Family stories say that Molly Bannaky taught Benjamin and his brothers and sisters how to read, using her bible as a lesson book. Benjamin eventually went to a school for boys, and according to family history, the schoolmaster changed Benjamin's last named to Banneker.

Molly had no way of knowing that something as small as a pail of milk would lead her to a new life in the new land of America. She was able to raise a family and run a farm on her own, as well as helping educate her children and grandchildren. And she would definitely have been proud to know that her grandson, Benjamin Banneker, would be remembered for the important part he played in American history.

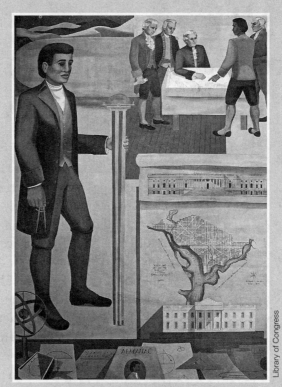

A mural of Benjamin Banneker in the Recorder of Deeds building in Washington, D.C.

Who Was Benjamin Banneker?

Molly Walsh Bannaky's grandson, Benjamin Banneker, loved mathematics, astronomy, and figuring out what made things work. When he was 21, he was given a pocket watch. He was fascinated by it, and finally he took it apart to see how it worked. Then Benjamin made his own clock, carved from wood. It was the first clock made in America that could strike the hour. Soon Benjamin was repairing clocks, as well as teaching himself about mathematics and astronomy. He built his own work cabin with a skylight where he could study the stars, and published his own almanac. Banneker also helped a friend, Major Andrew Ellicott, and the famous architect Pierre L'Enfant, who were surveying a new territory that would become the United States capital, Washington, D.C. When L'Enfant was fired because of his terrible temper, taking all the plans and surveys with him, Benjamin Banneker saved the day. He recreated all the plans from memory and saved the government from having the work done all over again. Today Benjamin Banneker is often remembered as the first black man of science.

PIGS AND PICKPOCKETS

It would be a shock to see farm animals roaming the streets of present-day Philadelphia, Pennsylvania. In the early 1700s, however, pigs, goats, and dogs freely wandered through that town eating garbage that had been dumped in the roads.

MUDDY STREETS, DIRTY FEET

Pretend you have been transported back in time. You are on a walking tour of Colonial Philadelphia three centuries ago. Tidy brick, stone, and wooden frame houses line the roads. With no sidewalks, you trudge through muddy, unpaved streets while dodging horses, wagons, pedestrians, and squealing pigs. You can smell the rotting garbage, which is attracting flies and roaches.

You notice that ladies are forced to hold up their long skirts and petticoats to avoid the dirt as they walk. Men pass by wearing knee-length coats and **breeches**. Many wear three-cornered hats, or "cocked hats" (today, we call them "tricorns"). Mud spatters their woolen stockings as they cross the street. You observe that by the time they are five years old, children are dressed like adults—from the square-toed shoes on their feet to the cocked hats on their heads.

STORES ON THE BOTTOM, HOMES ON THE TOP

You stroll by a merchant's red brick house trimmed with painted wood. It has an attic and windows that slide up and down. Without electricity, candles and oil lamps are used to light the four rooms inside, each of which has a fireplace for heat. The outhouse, called a "necessary," is behind the house. You can tell that many shop-keepers, like this one, have their stores on the first floor of their homes and living quarters on the second.

In the kitchen, you spot a woman preparing dinner for her family. She stirs a stew of meat and vegetables in a huge pot over the fire in the fireplace.

Many kinds of meat are available to the colonists, especially pork, poultry, **venison**, and fish. Corn, beans, squash, and pumpkins are plentiful, too. Thirsty adults and children drink beer, as well as cider and milk.

HARD AT WORK AND ACADEMICS

It appears to you that everyone in Colonial Philadelphia works hard, even children. Boys haul water from a nearby street well or water pump and help their fathers at their trades. Mothers teach their daughters to cook, sew, clean, and garden.

When you ask a friendly passerby about education, you are told that boys and girls have tutors at home or attend schools run by religious groups. Schools charge tuition for most but also teach a few poor students for free. Some wealthy young men even go to college. Some Philadelphians cannot afford schooling, however, and cannot read, so merchants hang up colorful pictures to show the products they are selling.

> **Breeches** are pants that reach just below the knee.
>
> **Venison** is deer meat.

Tanneries are businesses that convert animal hides into leather.

An **apprentice** is one who is bound to work for another for a certain amount of time in exchange for learning a trade.

Staves are strips of wood that form the sides of barrels.

Constables are law officers.

Brand means to mark with a hot iron.

MANY TRADES IN A BUSY CITY

What a noisy, lively town Philadelphia is, full of shops, offices, and bustling markets! Men work in stables, **tanneries**, lumberyards, and blacksmiths' shops. You stop to watch the glassmaker teach his **apprentice** how to make bottles by blowing melted glass through a long metal tube. Clockmakers, goldsmiths, potters, and other skilled craftsmen also are busy at work creating their goods. You learn that Philadelphia silversmiths and cabinetmakers are especially famous and export their wares to other places.

In the crowded market stalls, farmers sell sheep, pigs, and cows to the townspeople. Shoppers hurry to buy vegetables, fruits, and grains grown in the farmland surrounding Philadelphia. You pause to watch merchants and travelers gather at taverns to eat; play cards, chess, or backgammon; and discuss news and business.

Continuing your tour, you head toward the Delaware River, where you see dockworkers load ships with meat, grain, flour, and lumber products to be traded abroad for manufactured goods. Barrel **staves** are important exports. You notice that the shipbuilders are busy trying to keep up with the demand for more and bigger ships.

Watch out for pickpockets! **Constables** are patrolling, but sometimes crooks chase them away. Compared with other colonies, Philadelphia has a high rate of crime. While other colonies **brand** or fine criminals and turn them loose, Philadelphia imprisons lawbreakers in its sturdy jail.

TIME FOR WORSHIP AND LEISURE

Stopping to chat with a minister on the street, you are informed that Philadelphia is home to many religions, including Catholic, Anglican, Quaker, Lutheran, Presbyterian, Jewish, and Baptist. On days of worship, colonists dress in their best clothes and attend the church or synagogue of their choice.

For relaxation, you learn that on warm days, Philadelphians of all social positions enjoy swimming and fishing. In addition, men bowl and play billiards while women visit friends. Those who can afford horses love horseback or carriage riding. Horse-racing is especially popular, and colonists bet on their favorite horses. Dancing is another fun pastime for many men and women. In winter, you are told that for entertainment, Philadelphians ice-skate on frozen ponds and go sleighing.

Now, as you end your walk in this fast-growing town, imagine that by 1750 many of these streets will have sidewalks made of large slabs of slate. Posts will be set up along the edges to protect pedestrians from horse-and-carriage traffic. Merchants will use cobblestones to pave the roads in front of their shops, and whale-oil lamps will light those roads at night.

By 1774, Philadelphia will be the largest city in the colonies. In fact, it will be second only to London, England, as the most important English-speaking city in the world. Thanks to all this progress, on your next stroll around Philadelphia, you just might be able to keep your shoes out of the mud!

Aw, Go Fly a Kite!

So, what did kids like you do for fun in Colonial Philadelphia? You might be surprised to learn that many children played similar games to those you play today. For example, hopscotch, jump rope, chess, yo-yos, kite-flying, and marbles were enjoyed.

Children also played leapfrog — taking turns leaping over crouched-down friends. London Bridge was popular, too. A line of players walked between two children who joined hands above them while they all sang the nursery rhyme "London Bridge." The child who got "caught" at the end of the song by the hands being lowered sat out. This was repeated until all the children were "caught."

Dominoes were popular with French Philadelphians. The Dutch and English families were partial to skating. Badminton or shuttlecock was popular in England, and was played in the colonies, especially among the upper class. And you might recognize these games even though their names are not familiar: Jack straws was like today's pick up sticks, and knucklebones was a game similar to jacks.

By Ruth Spencer Johnson, sidebar by Janice Cole Gibson, illustrated by Mark Mitchell, *Cobblestone*, © by Carus Publishing Company. Reproduced with permission. May be reproduced for classroom use. *Toolkit Texts: Short Nonfiction for American History, Colonial Times* by Stephanie Harvey and Anne Goudvis, ©2014 (Portsmouth, NH: Heinemann).

Africans in New Amsterdam

The first Africans brought to the Dutch colony of New Netherland (present-day New York, New Jersey, and Delaware) arrived only a few years after the Dutch West India Company founded the settlement at New Amsterdam (present-day New York City) in 1624.

Before bringing Africans to New Amsterdam, the Dutch had brought "20, and odd Negroes" to Point Comfort (present-day Hampton) in Virginia.

They were captured by Dutch **privateers** from Portuguese slave ships carrying Africans from Angola, a country in East Africa, to the Spanish colonies in America.

During the 40 years that the Dutch held the colony, their ships delivered a few hundred Africans to the town. This delivery fulfilled a contract the West India Company had made with the settlers in 1629. The contract stated that the company would supply the settlers with slaves taken from vessels their company ships captured. In 1638, the company directors decided not to rely on capturing Africans being transported to America on ships, but to send their own ships to Africa and buy them there directly.

In 1655, the ship *Witte Paert* (*White Horse*) brought the first cargo of slaves from Allada (in present-day

> **Privateers**, in the sense used here, were ships that had a special license to attack enemy shipping and take their cargoes.

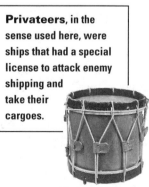

The Colonial Williamsburg Foundation

Library of Congress

Governor Kieft (right) and his colleagues review regulations governing the West India Company and its employees.

Benin, a country to the north of Angola) to New Amsterdam. Several more cargoes of Africans came to New Amsterdam before the English captured the town and renamed it New York in 1664.

Most of the Africans brought to New Amsterdam belonged to the West India Company. They lived together in a small village on the edge of Fresh Pond, near the site of the former World Trade Center. They worked to build and maintain the fort, load and unload ships, and do other maintenance work for the company. Their work was hard, as criminals were often sentenced to work with the "company's Negroes" as punishment for their misdeeds.

In 1643, Governor William Kieft granted a petition from 11 of the company slaves on behalf of themselves, their wives, and their children to be freed in recognition of their 18 or 19 years of service. Kieft also granted them titles to some of the land around their settlement. However, he did require that they pay a special rent, and he reserved the right to reenslave their children. In spite of these restrictions, many of the company's slaves gained their freedom and became landholders. One of them, Manuel de Gerrit de Reus, became

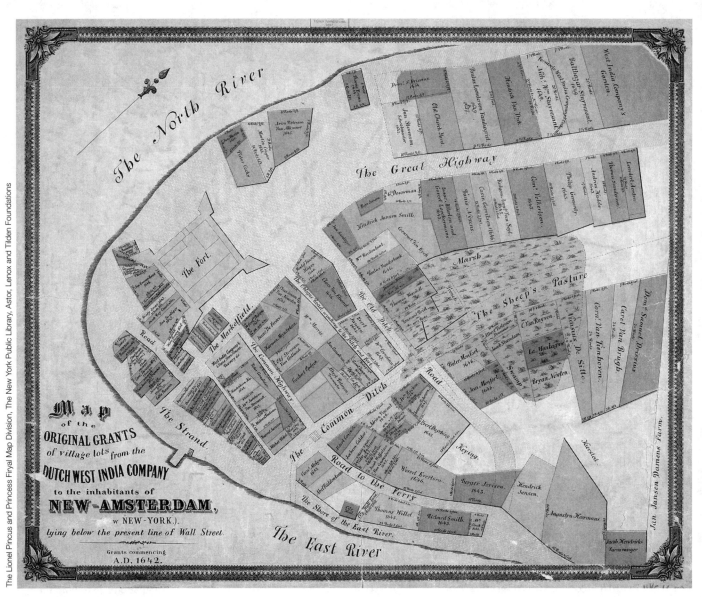

A map of the original grants of village lots from the Dutch West India Company to the residents of New Amsterdam.

the owner of what would become Washington Square, an important New York City landmark today.

Almost all the Africans who arrived before 1655 came from the Portuguese colony of Angola. Many of them were Catholics since, under Portuguese rule, the Catholic Church had been well established in Angola. Once in New York, however, many Africans joined the Dutch Reformed Church. About one-third of the marriages and baptisms recorded in that church were of Central Africans, whose homelands were recognized in their names. The

documents include, for example, the names Anthony Angola, Simon Congo, and Maria Angola. Their Christian background, it seems, might have helped many of these slaves gain their freedom, especially since there were Dutch who did not believe that it was right to hold a Christian in slavery past a certain time period. The latest arrivals, however, did not come from Christian areas, and they were quite numerous. As a result, after 1664, neither Dutch nor English masters were inclined to free them or to allow them to hold land.

"A Shelter for the poor and persecuted"

ROGER WILLIAMS

When I was unkindly and unchristianly, as I believe, driven from my house and land and wife and children (in the midst of New England winter, now 35 years past) at Salem, that ever-honored Governor Mr. Winthrop privately wrote to me to steer my course to Nahigonset-Bay and Indians for many high and heavenly and public ends, encouraging me [because of] the freeness of the place and from any English claims or patents. I took his prudent motion as a hint and voice from God and waving all other thoughts and motions, I steered my course from Salem (though in winter snow which I fell yet) unto these parts, wherein I may say I have seen the face of God.

I first pitched, and begun to build and plant at Sekonk, now Rehoboth, but I received a letter from my ancient friend Mr. Winslow, then Governor of Plymouth, professing his own and others love and respect to me, yet lovingly advising me, since I was fallen into the edge of their bounds and they were loath to displease the Bay, to remove but to the other side of the water and then he said I had the country free before me and might be as free as themselves and we should be loving neighbors together. These were the joint understandings of these two eminently wise and Christian Governors and others, in their day, together with their council and advice as to the freedom and vacancy of this place, which in this respect and many other Providences of the most holy and only wise, I called Providence.

Sometime after Plymouth, great Sachim Ousamagquin [Wampanoag chief Massasoit], upon occasion affirming that Providence was his land and therefore Plymouth's land and some resenting it, the then prudent and godly Governor Mr. Bradford and others of his godly council, answered that if after due examination it should be found true what the barbarian said, yet having, to my loss of a harvest that year, been now (though by their gentle advice) as good as banished from Plymouth as from the Massachusetts; and I had quietly and patiently departed from the, at their motion, to the place where now I was, I should not be molested and tossed up and down again while they had breath in their bodies; and surely between those my friends of the Bay and Plymouth, I was sorely tossed for fourteen weeks, in a bitter winter season, not knowing what bread or bed did mean; beside the yearly loss of no small matter in my trading with English and natives, being debarred from Boston, the chief mart and port of New England . . .

Upon frequent exceptions against Providence men that we had no authority for civil government, I went purposely to England and upon my report and petition, the Parliament granted us a charter of government for these parts, so judged vacant on all hands.

Here all over this colony, a great number of weak and distressed souls, scattered are flying hither from Old and New England, the Most High, and only wise hath in his infinite wisdom provided this country and this corner as a shelter for the poor and persecuted, according to their several persuasions . . .

We must part with lands and lives before we part with such a jewel.

"I WON'T GIVE UP"

Imagine your feelings if you and your family were captured, thrown into the dark hold of a ship, transported across the ocean, and forced to live and work in a totally new place. This is what happened to Nyack, the fictional African boy in this story.

APRIL 8, 1635 The name they call me here is Edward, but in our cabin at night, Momma still calls me Nyack. It means "won't give up." Papa named me in our African homeland 11 years ago.

In 1619, twenty captured Africans arrived in Jamestown. Historians believe they were treated as "bound laborers," like indentured servants. They probably worked for a set period of time and then were released from bondage. Only later were Africans enslaved and denied all freedoms.

Seldom were African parents and children captured and brought to America together, as Nyack's family was. More often a mother or father was dragged away from the rest of the family or a child was snatched from his or her parents.

APRIL 16, 1635 I haven't seen Papa since we were unloaded from the dark belly of the ship more than a week ago. Momma and I were taken away to work on a farm, and Papa was sent to another. The people in Jamestown have pale skin, and I can't understand a word they say.

MAY 4, 1635 We eat fish almost every night for dinner. The English women have taught Momma to make something called "biscuits." For breakfast, I pick berries and put them on my mush.

MAY 8, 1635 We live on a big farm. The master and his family live nearby. Momma has to go there every day to do work, like washing clothes and keeping the house clean. The people are teaching her to talk like they do, and they treat her kindly. But sometimes I hear her crying at night; I think she misses Papa as much as I do.

JUNE 14, 1635 There are many buildings at the farm. Servants cook, make clothes and tools, and build furniture. They also work in the gardens, take care of the animals, and hunt and fish. The biggest job of all is working in the tobacco fields. That's where I work every day. Sometimes I get tired, but I remember Papa's words—and my real name—and I don't give up.

JULY 10, 1635 Today, we walked two miles into town to go to church, and guess what? I saw Papa! He scooped me up in his arms and Momma just cried and hugged him.

JULY 24, 1635 Now Papa meets us at church each Sunday. Last week, he brought me a spinner toy that he made with a button and string. Today, he gave me three marbles he made out of clay. He tells me that one day, we'll live together again and go fishing like we used to back home.

JULY 30, 1635 We eat food from our garden every day now—corn and beans. My favorite treat is the young, sweet peas.

AUGUST 7, 1635 I get so hot and tired working in the tobacco field every day. We sing and tell stories while we work. I have to work hard, obey my master, and never give up.

AUGUST 23, 1635 I look forward to my Sunday trips. Since I've learned to count, I know that there are 22 houses in town, plus three stores and a church. Momma tells me that about 125 people live there with all their cows, pigs, and goats. There are nine boats down at the river. One of them is very big.

SEPTEMBER 1, 1635 Today, all the servants were given a new set of clothes and a pair of shoes for the coming year. I'm so happy to have a momma and papa who love me. They tell me to dream of whatever I want and never give up that dream.

By Janet Buckwalter, illustrated by Robin Hansen, *Appleseeds*, © by Carus Publishing Company. Reproduced with permission. May be reproduced for classroom use. *Toolkit Texts: Short Nonfiction for American History, Colonial Times* by Stephanie Harvey and Anne Goudvis, ©2014 (Portsmouth, NH: Heinemann).

Meet Thomas and Susannah Bridges

In the story of Thomas and Susannah Bridges, two fictional characters, you'll see that life in Jamestown was not easy, especially for orphans. (In the story, after the parents of Thomas and Susannah died, the children were indentured to Robert and Sarah Howell. In exchange for their work, they were given food and a place to live.)

20 May

This is the diary of Thomas Bridges, 10 years old in this year 1650. My parents and sister came from England, but I am Virginia-born. Father died fighting the Indians; Mother died of fever. Master Robert teaches me to brew the fine ale he serves in his **ordinary**, The Golden **Shallop**. He says it is more healthful to drink than the foul water of Jamestown, which sickens many.

> An **ordinary** was a place, similar to a tavern, that provided meals.
>
> A **shallop** was a type of boat that transported tobacco in Virginia waters.
>
> **Burgesses** were representatives in the colonial legislature, part of the governing body called the General Assembly.

21 May

This is the diary of Susannah Bridges, 13 years old in this year 1650. I sailed to Virginia when I was little. Now my brother and I are serving Master Robert Howell and Mistress Sarah, his wife, for seven years. I work with Mistress Sarah and watch her children, John, Anne, and Richard. Being nearly full-grown, I have many duties and not much time for writing. Thomas does not understand being indentured; he often plays.

No time yesterday for diary-keeping, as it was Monday and washday. Four **burgesses** stay in our sleeping room during the General Assembly's sessions. 'Tis hard to cook for guests and wash laundry all in the same day. Just hauling the water from the river took hours.

By K. Trippe-McRee, *Appleseeds*, © by Carus Publishing Company. Reproduced with permission.
Images: Jamestown Settlement History Museum, Williamsburg, Virginia. May be reproduced for classroom use. *Toolkit Texts: Short Nonfiction for American History, Colonial Times* by Stephanie Harvey and Anne Goudvis, ©2014 (Portsmouth, NH: Heinemann).

21 May
Chopped wood for Mistress Sarah to cook with in the big hearth. Helped Master Robert serve dinner. Burgesses stayed overlong for midday dinner. Mostly I like hearing their talk, but I wanted to go fishing with my friend Nicholas. Could not clear tables till they left. Caught two fine bass trout for Mistress Sarah's fish stew. Saw a ship with tall sails newly arrived from England!

22 May
Cold stew at breakfast so Mistress Sarah and I could start early, baking bread. We made several loaves with English white flour. Mistress Sarah let me taste the bread. It is so different from our Virginia corn bread! Thomas was slow in bringing wood. He forgets we are servants now.

22 May
Brought wood for kitchen and alehouse fires. Played games. Chopped more wood. Took a letter to burgesses staying at Master Richard Wright's. Nicholas and I went to watch ships being loaded with tobacco for England. Master Robert boxed my ears for neglecting my work.

23 May
Our one sleeping room above the ordinary needed sweeping after four men stayed there. Also weeded Master Robert's garden. Thomas helped, then ran off with Nicholas. He returned with berries from Mistress Wright, Nicholas's mother. Though I took longer at weeding without Thomas's help, Mistress Sarah taught me to make piecrust with English flour. Had my first taste of berry pie. It was so sweet and fine!

By K. Trippe-McRee, *Appleseeds*, © by Carus Publishing Company. Reproduced with permission.
Images: Jamestown Settlement History Museum, Williamsburg, Virginia. May be reproduced for classroom use. *Toolkit Texts: Short Nonfiction for American History, Colonial Times* by Stephanie Harvey and Anne Goudvis, ©2014 (Portsmouth, NH: Heinemann).

23 May

Went hunting with Master Robert and shot two rabbits for stew. Saw three hogs foraging in the woods. I am glad we do not chase them for butchering till fall. Walked to the orchard. This season, Master Robert's trees bear apples for cider, which I will learn to make. Hoed all of the garden and read extra Bible verses, as I neglect my work.

24 May

Helped with mending today after cooking was done. Then Mistress Sarah set me to hemming. She says my stitching improves. Played with her little ones till supper.

24 May

Went to brew house to fill pitchers of ale for dinner, then helped Master Robert with accounts. Gave me extra sums, because I must learn if I am to keep an ordinary someday. I would rather go fishing with Nicholas and pretend to drill like the men mustered for the militia.

25 May

Burgesses departed today. I swept and aired their sleeping room. Extra cooking as tomorrow is Sunday.

25 May

Extra wood needed as tomorrow is Sunday. Weeded rest of garden. Master Robert taught me and John to play Thirty-And-One with waxed cards newly come from England. The numbers on the cards must add up to thirty-and-one. I think Master Robert seeks to teach sums, but 'tis fun to add cards.

26 May

Church. Stayed after to talk with Rebecca and Jane, servants to Mistress Wright. Practiced reading the Bible with Mistress Sarah. She says I must read better, so I may teach my children to read the Bible someday. 'Tis pleasant to sit quietly all day after church with no work to do. Washday again on the morrow.

26 May

Fell asleep in church. Master Robert poked me. To improve my reading, Master Robert gave me many Bible verses to study. I hate Sundays as I must sit inside. Nicholas and I go fishing again tomorrow.

Playtime

Though English children didn't have much free time, like Thomas and Susannah, they sometimes had time for games. One game was called Prisoners' Base. Players chose sides and marked boundaries for their territory. The area between lines was No Man's Land. Players could tag opponents in No Man's Land and put them in "prison" (an area along their boundary line). Tagged players waited there until freed by teammates. Clever prisoners formed a chain. When a teammate tagged the chain's end, all prisoners in the chain were free. The game ended when all players from one side were captured or when one player managed to enter the opposing side's empty prison.

By K. Trippe-McRee, *Appleseeds*, © by Carus Publishing Company. Reproduced with permission.
Images: Jamestown Settlement History Museum, Williamsburg, Virginia. May be reproduced for classroom use. *Toolkit Texts: Short Nonfiction for American History, Colonial Times* by Stephanie Harvey and Anne Goudvis, ©2014 (Portsmouth, NH: Heinemann).

JAMESTOWN KIDS

LIFE WAS HARSH, BUT THERE WERE SOME FUN TIMES.

Children, both European and Indian, served as ambassadors and interpreters between the colonists and the Powhatans, the Indians of coastal Virginia. During the colony's first 17 years, hundreds of children arrived at Jamestown, many of them unaccompanied by their parents on the transatlantic voyage.

In 17th-century England, children were sometimes separated from their families at an early age. They were sent, on a regular basis, to live with relatives for their education. Many had lost one or both parents to plague or malaria. Orphaned children were assigned duties as pages or maids in their new homes, and often their masters assumed the role of parent and teacher. Out of necessity, many children accompanied their masters and mistresses when they traveled, even when it meant a 3,000-mile transatlantic journey.

CHILD EXCHANGE

Some young boys, who had been sent to work on ships as servants to ship masters, rose through the ranks to become sea captains. One was Christopher Newport, who started his career as a ship apprentice. He then worked his way up and was named commander of the 1607 expedition to Jamestown.

Samuel Collier, Richard Mutton, James Brumfield, and Nathaniel Peacock were the first boys to arrive at Jamestown in 1607. At the time, Virginia was not a healthy or safe place for young children. According to John Smith, the leader of the Jamestown colony, two boys died within months of their arrival. Samuel Collier survived to serve as Smith's page and accompanied him during meetings with Powhatan, the ruler of the Powhatan people until his death in 1618.

Smith saw Collier as young and easily able to adapt to new surroundings. Therefore, he sent him to live with the Powhatans to learn their language. In time, Collier's knowledge of the Powhatan language and customs allowed him to act as a trusted communicator between the English and the Virginia Indians. Many of the children sent to live among the Indians, however, became confused about their cultural identity and were torn between colonial interests and Indian life ways.

Powhatan children also served as liaisons. Powhatan sent Indian children to James Fort with food and messages for the colonists. In 1608, the young Indian Namontack was sent to live at James Fort in exchange for the English boy Thomas Savage, who lived with Powhatan for three years. Namontack learned the English language and even traveled to England with Christopher Newport. Pocahontas, one of Powhatan's youngest and most favored children, served as Powhatan's messenger to the colonists. She learned the English language and became a follower of the Christian faith. In 1614, she married colonist John Rolfe.

Left: Pocahontas, the favorite daughter of the Indian chief who befriended the Jamestown settlers, later married colonist John Rolfe and visited England with him. She never returned, dying there at the age of 22.

Right: Shell earrings that are believed to have belonged to Pocahontas.

© Joseph Sohm–Visions of America/ Stockbyte/Getty Images/HIP

Preservation Virginia

The Art Gallery Collection/Alamy

Left, top: This lead figurine of a boy may have been a toy or a trade item.

Left, bottom: A section of a recorder, a common musical instrument.

Right: Men and women, of all levels of society in Jamestown and in Europe, enjoyed bowling in the 1600s. The men in this painting are playing skittles, a type of bowling game that used nine wooden pins as the target.

CHORE LIST

Ann Burras, a 13-year-old maid to Mistress Fox, arrived in the colony in 1608, on the ship Mary and Margaret. It was English custom to send young girls to work in the homes of wealthy relatives or friends in order to receive a proper education and upbringing. Young girls were trained in hand knitting, lace making, and stocking knitting. Both boys and girls helped with such household tasks as fetching water, finding fuel for fires, milking, preparing food, and washing. Shortly after arriving at Jamestown, Ann married colonist John Layden.

Some children on the voyage to Virginia accompanied their parents. The sisters Elizabeth, Mary, and Margaret Gates traveled to Virginia in 1611 with their mother and father, Sir Thomas Gates. In the cramped quarters of the small ships, the transatlantic voyage was difficult, and disease and food shortages were common. The girls' mother died during the voyage, and Sir Thomas Gates, knowing that the environment of the colony was not safe or healthy for the motherless girls, sent them home to England the following year.

FOOTBALL, ANYONE?

Jamestown life, however, was not all work. There are written accounts of European and Indian children playing bowling games and football. The aim of Indian football was to kick, rather than throw, a leather ball to a goal. Players were not allowed to fight, pull, or knock one another down during the game. John Smith writes much about Pocahontas playing and turning cartwheels in James Fort. These surviving accounts make it easy to imagine children playing together in the streets of Jamestown.

Whether at play or at work, the children of Jamestown were instrumental in sustaining the Virginia colony. They were part of the colony's first interaction with the Indians, and they symbolized the hope of the colonists and the Virginia Indians that trust would grow and endure between them.

A GIFT OF FRIENDSHIP

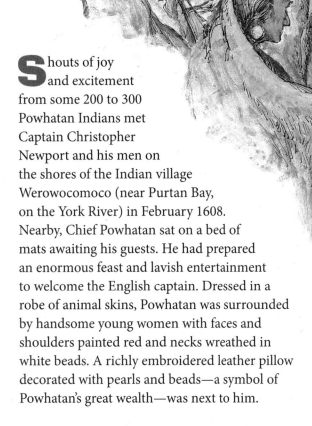

Shouts of joy and excitement from some 200 to 300 Powhatan Indians met Captain Christopher Newport and his men on the shores of the Indian village Werowocomoco (near Purtan Bay, on the York River) in February 1608. Nearby, Chief Powhatan sat on a bed of mats awaiting his guests. He had prepared an enormous feast and lavish entertainment to welcome the English captain. Dressed in a robe of animal skins, Powhatan was surrounded by handsome young women with faces and shoulders painted red and necks wreathed in white beads. A richly embroidered leather pillow decorated with pearls and beads—a symbol of Powhatan's great wealth—was next to him.

A Relationship Is Established

When the Englishmen arrived, Powhatan offered them food and drink. The two groups spent the rest of the day establishing friendly relations.

The following day, to show his sincerity, the chief presented Newport with an assortment of gifts. Newport reciprocated with

a gift that amazed the chief: With great ceremony, a boy was introduced to Powhatan as the captain's son, Thomas Newport, and then given to the chief. Several days later, Powhatan responded by giving his own trusty servant, Namontack, to Newport. These acts sealed the leaders' friendship.

An English Boy in a Native World

The English boy, whose last name was Savage, was not Newport's son. Just 13 years old, Thomas had left his home in Cheshire, England, and traveled to London to join Newport's first supply expedition to the New World. After a three-month voyage, he had arrived in Virginia on January 2, 1608. A little more than a month since landing at Jamestown, Thomas found himself in Werowocomoco amid hundreds of natives with whom he had nothing in common.

This may not have been as bad as it seems, however. After all, life in Jamestown was anything but easy. Only about one-third of the original 104 settlers were alive. In addition, a fire had swept through Jamestown, devouring every barrel of recently delivered supplies and all but three huts. Now the settlement's survival depended on Newport's ability to make peace with the Indians and enlist their help in obtaining food.

At Werowocomoco, on the other hand, there was plenty of food, warmth, and shelter. Powhatan quickly grew fond of Thomas, and in only a few months, the boy had learned enough Algonquian to serve as a messenger and interpreter between the English and the Indians. But while he was with the Indians, relations between the two groups became increasingly uncomfortable as more white settlers arrived in Virginia. Powhatan moved farther inland to distance his people from the English, but the Europeans kept coming.

The Trust Is Broken

Actually, both sides were guilty of straining the friendship. The English stole corn and other food supplies from the Indians, and the Indians ambushed the English for their tools and weapons. The conflict finally erupted in the winter of 1609–1610 when Powhatan's men killed an English trading party. Thomas, by then 15, left Powhatan and made his way back to Jamestown.

But Thomas continued to serve as an interpreter, and he negotiated trade deals with the various tribes. Thomas also explored the Rappahannock and Potomac rivers and the Eastern Shore of Virginia. The Accomack Indian chief Esmy Shichans granted Thomas thousands of acres of land, making him one of the first permanent English settlers on Virginia's Eastern Shore.

ON THE BACKS OF LABORERS

Jamestown Settlement History Museum

This indenture made the Fourth Day of August in the year of our Lord 1620 between Thomas Harmon of Derby, laborer, aged twenty years, of the one Party, and Arthur Manley of London, Esq. of the other Party, Whitnesseth that the said Thomas Harmon, for the Considerations here in after Mentioned, does by these present covenant, bargain and bind himself to serve the foresaid Arthur Manley, his heirs and assigns and to be by him sent unto the Country and land of Virginia, in the parts beyond the Seas and employed upon his plantation there, for the space of Four years, during which the said Thomas Harmon shall truly employ himself to the utmost of his power, knowledge and skill to perform true and faithful service unto the said Arthur Manley his heirs and assigns in all such Labor and business as he or they shall think good to use and employ him the said Thomas Harmon in.

The success of the new colony at Jamestown hinged on many factors, none more important than the need for a large labor force. Adventure and the prospect of opportunity were what originally attracted English men and women to leave home and cross the ocean to Virginia. Later, especially after tobacco took off, a number of young people agreed to work as indentured servants for a specific amount of time in exchange for passage to the New World, food, and clothing.

Top: Growing tobacco took a lot of workers. At first, the workers in Virginia's fields were indentured Englishmen. Later, Africans made up the majority of the work force, and were eventually forced into slavery. Bottom: An indenture.

INDENTURED SERVITUDE

An indenture was a written contract between a servant and a master. By 1618, servants in Virginia were promising to work for a master for a period of four to seven years, after which they would be free. At the end of the predetermined time, servants were given three barrels of corn and a new suit of clothes. Sometimes they also received land, livestock, tools, and money, depending on how their indenture had been negotiated.

The first servants were employed to clear land, build structures, grow crops, and hunt for food. Servants, like all settlers, lived under strict laws. They could not plant their own crops or return to their homeland. Those who disobeyed could be whipped.

Some servants arrived in the New World already planning not to fulfill their contracts and so immediately ran away from their masters. Others became disenchanted with the hard life and fell into drunkenness, threatened their masters, destroyed tools and stores, or committed suicide. And the truth is that many masters were not easy to work for, nor were they all fair. They abused their servants and made them live under harsh conditions.

In time, land began to be allotted to settlers according to the number of people they brought to Virginia. This system, called *headright*, encouraged the use of servants, which, in turn, created a whole new industry in England: Merchants and ships' captains were hired to recruit people for service in the colony.

Many young men and women, **naïve** to the harsh life in the New World, placed themselves into **bondage**. Others were forced into servitude: English officials sometimes sentenced debtors, political prisoners, and criminals to terms as laborers in Virginia.

> **Naïve** means lacking the ability to be critical or analytical.
>
> **Bondage** is the state of being bound as a servant or slave.

Jamestown Settlement History Museum

Making a meal was no simple task in colonial times. Indentured servants worked long hours, some indoors and some in the fields, to meet their masters' needs.

Building permanent homes at Jamestown required bricks, which had to be molded by hand and baked in ovens.

A **man-of-war** is a combat ship.

Chattel is personal, movable property.

FAST FACT

A FORM OF SERVITUDE HAD EXISTED IN ENGLAND SINCE THE MIDDLE AGES (476–1453): WORKERS THERE USUALLY CONTRACTED WITH AN EMPLOYER FOR A YEAR OR SERVED A MULTIYEAR APPRENTICESHIP.

AFRICANS ARRIVE

Then, in August 1619, an English **man-of-war** arrived in Virginia. On board were about 20 Africans from Angola, a Portuguese colony in Africa, who may have been sold as indentured servants upon their arrival in Virginia. Because records are few and incomplete, it is unknown how many of these Africans were released from this servitude. It is known that some free black colonists lived in Virginia during the 17th century.

Over the next several decades, some former African servants acquired property, and at least one owned slaves. Marriage between blacks and whites existed, and free Africans had access to the courts. Although no voting records survive, it is believed that free African males who owned land may have voted in elections for the House of Burgesses.

FROM SERVITUDE TO SLAVERY

Most English settlers viewed the Africans as inferior, however, and the rights of black people quickly eroded. By the 1660s, the General Assembly had acknowledged the existence of lifetime slavery. By 1725, laws that stripped slaves of most basic rights had been passed. Under slavery, Africans were considered **chattel** that could be bought and sold.

As Africans became the main source of labor, indentured service faded away. Some historians believe that early colonists regarded the Africans as less than human, which allowed them to justify enslaving them. Others suggest that the English simply were following the lead of other slave-holding countries, such as Spain and Portugal. Still others add that slavery was due to economics: With the growth of the tobacco industry, the demand for cheap labor increased, and slavery was less costly than indentured service.

By the turn of the 18th century, transplanted Africans who were forced into slavery made up a growing part of Virginia's population. Initially in Virginia, the labor of the first indentured servants allowed the colony to prosper. Later, the institution of slavery became the foundation of the plantation economy in Virginia.

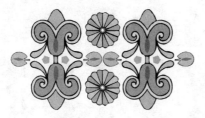

The First Poles in America

By Nancy Day

As the English made plans to colonize Virginia in the late 1500s, they realized that the area's natural resources could be used to produce pitch, tar, and other products used in England's shipbuilding industry. But the colony would need people who knew how to make these substances from the New World's raw materials. As early as 1585, Richard Hakluyt, an English geographer experienced in overseas trade, looked to Poland as a source of skilled labor for these purposes.

The first Polish immigrants to the New World—known as Poles, Polanders, or Polonians—arrived in Jamestown in October 1608 aboard English captain Christopher Newport's second supply ship, the Mary and Margaret. The Poles immediately went to work making pitch, tar, and *soapashes* for export.

The skills the Poles brought with them were so important to the success of the Jamestown settlement that the Virginia Company of London made sure that these workers trained apprentices. The company's records explained, ". . . because their skill in making pitch and tarr and sope-ashees shall not dye with them, it is agreed that some young men, shalbe put unto them to learne their skill and knowledge therein for the benefitt of the Country hereafter."

In 1619, the Poles objected to the colony's law that only natives of England were allowed to vote. The records of the Virginia Company from July 21, 1619, show that their protest was successful: "Upon some dispute of the Polonians resident in Virginia, it was now agreed (notwithstanding any former order to the contrary) that they shalbe enfranchized, and made as free as any inhabitant there whatsoever."

Thus, the first Poles in America are remembered for the qualities in which Americans always have taken great pride: hard work, helping others, and exercising a basic right of all citizens—the right to vote.

Soapashes are the first step in making an early form of soap—made from wood ash and animal fat.

FAST FACT

SOME HISTORIANS HAVE SUGGESTED THAT THE POLES DUG THE FIRST FRESHWATER WELL AND PLAYED THE FIRST "BAT-BALL" GAMES AT JAMESTOWN. BECAUSE OF THE SCARCE RECORDS AVAILABLE FROM THOSE EARLY DAYS, HOWEVER, THESE ACCOUNTS CANNOT BE CONFIRMED.

TSENACOMOCO MY WORLD

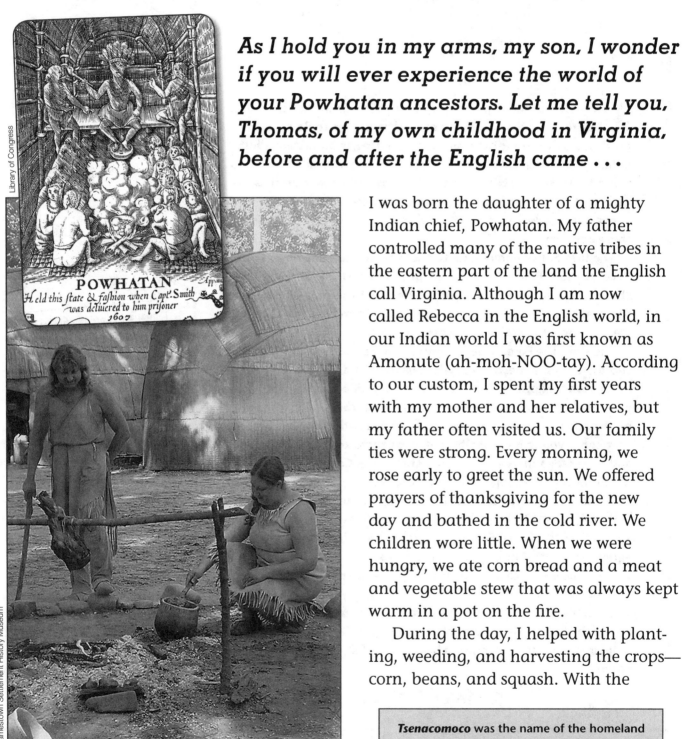

Library of Congress

POWHATAN

Held this state & fashion when Capt. Smith
was deliuered to him prifoner
1607

Appama

Jamestown Settlement History Museum

Native American interpreters reenact the Powhatan
way of life at Jamestown settlement.

As I hold you in my arms, my son, I wonder if you will ever experience the world of your Powhatan ancestors. Let me tell you, Thomas, of my own childhood in Virginia, before and after the English came . . .

I was born the daughter of a mighty Indian chief, Powhatan. My father controlled many of the native tribes in the eastern part of the land the English call Virginia. Although I am now called Rebecca in the English world, in our Indian world I was first known as Amonute (ah-moh-NOO-tay). According to our custom, I spent my first years with my mother and her relatives, but my father often visited us. Our family ties were strong. Every morning, we rose early to greet the sun. We offered prayers of thanksgiving for the new day and bathed in the cold river. We children wore little. When we were hungry, we ate corn bread and a meat and vegetable stew that was always kept warm in a pot on the fire.

During the day, I helped with planting, weeding, and harvesting the crops—corn, beans, and squash. With the

Tsenacomoco was the name of the homeland that the Powhatan shared with other Native American tribes for generations.

By Julie Durwa, *Appleseeds*, © by Carus Publishing Company. Reproduced with permission.
May be reproduced for classroom use. *Toolkit Texts: Short Nonfiction for American History, Colonial Times*
by Stephanie Harvey and Anne Goudvis, ©2014 (Portsmouth, NH: Heinemann).

other girls and women, I gathered wild berries, nuts, and greens. This was our work. The boys hunted and fished with the men and practiced to become warriors.

Women also built our homes. We bent young trees—saplings—into a frame, then covered it with mats that we wove from reeds. Our homes were movable. We carried them from place to place during deer hunting season. The other girls and I learned to weave, because we needed new reed mats every few months.

Inside our home, our yehakin, it was dark and snug. We stored our belongings in baskets that hung from the walls. The fire in the center kept our home warm in the winter, and the smoke kept out bugs in the summer. We slept on platforms covered with deerskins and other furs.

I was never lonely as a child, for there were always family members around. We did everything together. In the evenings, our elders shared stories and songs. Often, we danced late into the night. I learned much through listening, watching, and working with my mother and her family.

Jamestown Settlement History Museum (top and bottom)

WHAT'S IN A NAME?

Powhatan or *Powhatans:*

Both are correct.

Powhatan was the name of Pocahontas's father. He was the leader of the *Powhatans,* a tribe of the Virginia Indians.

Scribner's Popular History of the United States, by William Cullen Bryant, 1896

King Powhatan *comands C.Smith to be slayne his daughter* Pokahontas *beggs his life his thankfullnefs and how he Subicoted 39 of their kings readeg hiftory*

When I was about 8 years old, I went to live with my father (your grandfather), Chief Powhatan. I soon became my father's favorite daughter. I had grown into a strong, sturdy girl, with an independent streak. My father nicknamed me Pocahontas, which means "little mischievous one." In my father's village, I observed the coming and going of important people. Powhatan often hosted large feasts, which I helped prepare.

When I was 11, the English came to our land. They had traveled across the great water with the hope of finding a new land filled with riches. Instead, they found many hardships. Without enough food and supplies, they suffered greatly from hunger and sickness. Many of them died. That was the English year 1607.

My father was unsure if the English were friends or foes. They brought no women or children, as if they planned to make war. And they built a fort around their settlement. It was a dilemma for my father—should he consider the English his friends, or go to war against them?

I first met Captain John Smith when my father's warriors captured him. He was a powerful leader of the English, and our people respected him for his bravery. The Powhatan holy men declared him to be our friend. During a special ceremony, Captain Smith came to believe that I saved him from being put to death by my father. In fact, it was Powhatan who made the decision to treat Captain Smith as an adopted son. (As a young girl, I had little power over what happened to anyone.) Captain Smith was released, and my father gave food to the settlers. He helped them survive.

Though I was but a child, and Captain Smith was a grown man and a foreigner, we became friends. He treated me kindly and gave me gifts of beads. But when I visited the Jamestown settlement, I didn't go to see Captain Smith—I mostly spent time playing with the young boys there.

As time passed, the friendship between my father and the English began to fall apart. Captain Smith did not act the way an adopted son should; he went against my father's wishes and continued to build his settlement, called Jamestown. It was now clear to Powhatan that the English wanted his land for their own. In the year 1613, the English captured me. They held me against my will for one whole year, hoping to make my father change his mind. But it didn't work.

An engraved portrait of Captain John Smith, an English soldier, explorer, and author.

During that year, I fell in love with your father, an Englishman named John Rolfe. Though I already had an Indian husband, John asked my father for his permission to marry me. When Powhatan agreed, it was the end of my life as I had known it. John Rolfe and I were married in 1614.

I see now that the English changed the way of life for my people. There is less land for the Powhatan people to farm, so they cannot always sustain themselves in the old ways. They have begun to depend on the English for food and trade goods. Sickness and death have done terrible things to my people, the result of diseases brought by the English. I fear that the world of my childhood is gone forever.

A lithograph (below) depicting the large gathering of Native Americans and Englishmen for the wedding of Pocahontas and John Rolfe, an English tobacco farmer, in Jamestown in spring 1614.

Library of Congress

The Kobal Collection at Art Resource, NY

Thomas Rolfe

Pocahontas and John Rolfe had a son they named Thomas. He was born in 1615. The next year, Thomas traveled to England with his parents. After Pocahontas's death in 1617, baby Thomas stayed in England to be raised by his uncle. John Rolfe went back to Virginia and died before his son finally returned in 1635. In Virginia, Thomas Rolfe became a wealthy landowner, married, and had one daughter. He never met his grandfather, Powhatan, and he lived his life as an Englishman.

TIMELINE of the Life of POCAHONTAS

Pocahontas

1595

Pocahontas, the daughter of Chief Powhatan, is born.

April 1607

Jamestown is founded.

May 1607

Pocahontas visits Jamestown and meets Captain John Smith, whom she tutors in the Powhatan's language. Pocahontas and John Smith become friends.

December 1607

Smith is captured by Powhatan warriors and taken to meet Powhatan. Pocahontas saves Smith from mock "execution," staged as part of a ceremony intended to adopt the Englishman into the Powhatan tribes.

Statue of Captain John Smith

January 1608

Pocahontas sends Indian messengers to Jamestown with food for the struggling colonists.

January 1608

Powhatan orders Smith's death; Pocahontas warns Smith of her father's decree, allowing him to escape from the assassins.

October 1609

Injured in a gunpowder accident, Smith leaves Virginia and returns to England for good.

April 1613

Pocahontas is kidnapped by Captain Samuel Argall, who takes her to Jamestown as an English prisoner and holds her for ransom.

Baptism of Pocahontas

September 1613

Pocahontas is baptized by a Protestant minister and changes her name to Rebecca.

April 1614

Pocahontas marries colonist John Rolfe.

June 1616

Pocahontas visits England and meets the king. She also meets Smith again.

March 1617

Pocahontas dies (possibly from pneumonia) in Gravesend, England, and is buried March 21. Her son Thomas stays in England until early adulthood.

Statue of Pocahontas

TRADING BOYS, TRADING CULTURES

Have you ever traded something with a friend? Can you imagine what it would be like if YOU were the thing being traded? That is what happened to a real Jamestown boy, Thomas Savage. When Tom was 13, he went to Jamestown with the First Supply ship. Not long after he arrived, he was traded to the Powhatan Indians for an Indian boy named Namontack. The year was 1608. Imagine what Tom Savage might have had to say about his adventure . . .

Captain Smith and Captain Newport took me to a meeting with Chief Powhatan in February. Captain Newport gave some gifts to the Chief, but the Chief wasn't happy, because the gifts didn't include guns. Wanting to prove their friendship, the captains offered Captain Newport's "son" instead. Imagine my surprise when I realized they were talking about me! They told Powhatan that I could live with him and his people to learn their language if, in exchange, Powhatan would let them take one of his sons to learn about the English. Powhatan agreed and sent Namontack, who was actually his trusted

FAST FACT

IN JANUARY 1608, CAPTAIN NEWPORT BROUGHT 80-100 NEW COLONISTS AND SUPPLIES TO JAMESTOWN. THIS WAS CALLED THE FIRST SUPPLY.

servant, not his son. Powhatan also gave Captain Newport some baskets of beans. I could hardly believe that I had been traded for another boy and some beans!

I was scared when I was left with the Powhatans, but they were kind to me. About a month later, the Chief decided to send me back to Jamestown to find out what the English were planning to do. Soon, however, he changed his mind and wanted me to come back. I ended up staying with the Powhatans for two years and became an expert at their language. The Chief relied on me as a messenger and interpreter and became fond of me. I finally left when the fighting between the colonists and the Indians became so bad that I feared for my life.

When I first went to live with the Powhatans, Captain Newport took Namontack to England.

There, he introduced Namontack
as a Virginia prince. Captain Newport
made this up to impress people in England.
He wanted to get more support for the
Jamestown settlement.

Namontack was treated well in England. He
must have been amazed by the English way of life
and the huge population. When he returned to his
people several months later, he told the Chief about
everything he had seen. The Chief refused to believe that
the colonists belonged to such a powerful nation.

I wasn't the only English boy given to the Powhatan tribe.
Captain Smith traded a young man named Henry Spelman to the
Powhatans in 1609. Unlike me, Henry knew how to read and write. He
later wrote about the Powhatans and their way of life. I have a feeling
that people will still be reading Henry's words many years in the future.
I wonder if anyone will read about me?

Safe Haven in Florida

October 1687: Twelve exhausted Africans reach the town of St. Augustine, Florida, after escaping from bondage in South Carolina.

These eight men, three women, and one three-year-old were the first of many enslaved Africans who fled to Spanish Florida from the English colonies in the Carolinas. As the number of fugitives grew, King Charles II of Spain officially declared in 1693 that runaways who reached Florida and converted to Catholicism would be given liberty, "so that by their example and by my liberality others will do the same." The first "underground railroad" to freedom for enslaved people in America had begun, and it traveled from north to south and had American Indian "conductors."

By 1738, enough former slaves had made their way to St. Augustine to form a **militia** regiment. That same year, the Spanish established a village for these freedmen. Called Gracia Real de Santa Teresa de Mose, it was located about two miles north of Castillo (Castle) de San Marcos, which was connected to St. Augustine by a tidal creek. The first settlers— 38 men and their families—farmed the area and provided a northern defense line against possible British attack. To supplement the food the settlers obtained by farming, hunting, and fishing, the royal storehouse handed out food rations. The village had a church and a Catholic priest who

Fort Mose's soldiers had uniforms that were similar to these worn by Cuban troops in the 1700s. Thirty-eight men, most of them married, formed the Fort Mose militia and lived at the fort.

Oficial *Soldado*

served the newly escaped slaves and provided instruction in Catholicism.

A small fort was constructed at the village, but Mose, as the settlement was called, and its fort existed for less than two years. When the English attacked St. Augustine in 1740, the Spaniards evacuated the people of Mose to the safety of the Castillo de

A militia is an army of volunteer citizens rather than expert soldiers.

The Colonial Williamsburg Foundation

Courtesy of the Florida Museum of Natural History—Historical Archaeology Collections

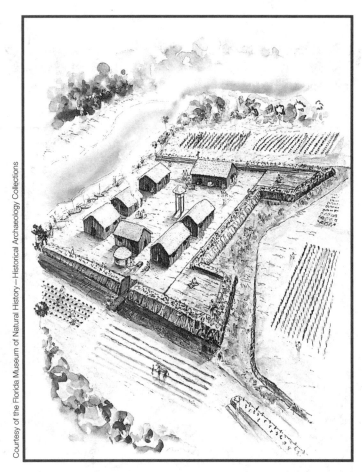

An artist reconstructed how the town at Fort Mose probably looked, using surviving documents and uncovered architectural remains as guides.

San Marcos. Soon after, the English occupied Fort Mose. The Spanish troops, including about 20 free black soldiers, surprised the English and drove them away in a fierce battle that destroyed what was left of the fort. Twelve years later, both Fort Mose and the town were rebuilt.

Then, in 1985, through a combination of satellite imagery provided by the National Aeronautics and Space Administration (NASA), analysis of 18th-century maps, and a series of core drillings in the marsh, archaeologists discovered and confirmed the location of the second fort. For three years, University of Florida archaeologists excavated the area. The finds revealed that the fort was a large, three-sided structure, with the side facing the river open and unprotected. The defensive walls were built of earth faced with marsh clay. A moat surrounded the fort, and it was filled with prickly-pear cactus and Spanish bayonets—an effective protection against invaders.

Inside the fort were a watchtower, a church, and the houses of the residents. In 1759, there were 22 households and 67 residents, including 37 men, 15 women, and 15 children. The leader of the community, Francisco Menéndez (see next page), was the captain of the black regiment. Some refugees had married each other; others married free or enslaved blacks in St. Augustine or Indians. Their houses were described as palm thatch huts "like those of the Indians." Archaeologists have shown that they were oval in shape and spanned 12 to 20 feet in diameter.

An Unwelcomed Peace

Mose was a community of many languages and cultures. Some residents, like Menéndez, had lived in Africa, and various African, Spanish, English,

Much of what we know about Fort Mose comes from 200-year-old historical documents in the archives of Seville, Spain. Excavations at Fort Mose are greatly expanding the information found in these records. They have revealed the details of life in the town and fort and even allowed archaeologists to reconstruct how the area may have looked. Mose stands as a monument to the courage of black Americans who risked, and often lost, their lives in the long struggle to achieve freedom.

and Indian languages were probably all spoken at Mose. Excavations have recovered Spanish, local Indian, and English pottery used in the households of the town, along with wine bottles and tobacco pipes. Gun flints, musket balls, and uniform buttons reflect the community's military flavor, while other buttons, pins, and thimbles suggest that European-style clothing was worn and made there. Excavations have also uncovered a St. Christopher medal and a bead that might have come from a rosary. These were probably the possessions of a new Catholic convert.

Mose was abandoned as a black community in 1763—the same year the war known as the French and Indian War in the Americas ended. The Treaty of Paris gave Florida to England. All of the inhabitants of the Spanish colony, including the people of Mose, left their homes and sailed to Cuba. Once again, they had to start a new life in an unfamiliar land.

Francisco Menéndez

Who was Francisco Menéndez? Like many other blacks in St. Augustine, he was a slave in South Carolina who escaped to Florida. As a subject of the King of Spain, who controlled Florida, he was given his freedom. Menéndez was appointed leader of the black militia at Fort Mose. Soon he was leading raids into South Carolina. After Fort Mose was destroyed in the battle between the English and the Spanish, Menéndez became a sailor on a Spanish ship that raided British ships. He was captured by the British and sold back into slavery, but he either escaped or the Spanish paid a ransom for his return to Florida. There he was asked to help rebuild Fort Mose. He stayed there until 1763, when the British took control of Fort Mose. Menéndez moved to Cuba with the rest of the Fort Mose community. They established a new settlement there. Menéndez is thought to have died in Havana, Cuba.

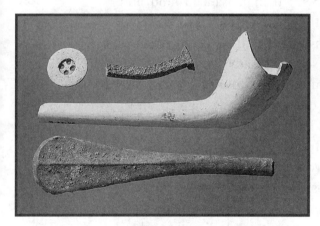

Above: Just a few of the many finds uncovered at Fort Mose: button, nail, pipe bowl and stem, and utensil handle.

Right: To tell the story of those who lived at Fort Mose, a video documentary was made with reenactors taking the part of escaped slaves seeking safety at the fort.

Courtesy of the Florida Museum of Natural History—Historical Archaeology Collections (left and right)

Struggling to settle Jamestown

JOHN SMITH

The first land we made, we fell with Cape Henry, the very mouth of the Bay of Chesapeake, which at the present we little expected having by a cruel storm been put to the northward. Anchoring in this bay, twenty or thirty went ashore with the Captain, and in coming aboard they were assaulted with certain Indians which charged them within pistolshot, in which conflict Captain Archer and Mathew Morton were shot. Whereupon Captain Newport, seconding them, but having spent their arrows retired without harm. And in that place was the box opened wherein the Council for Virginia was nominated. And arriving at the place where now seated, the Council was sworn and the president elected…where was made choice for our situation and a very fit place for the erecting of a great city. All our provision was brought ashore, and with as much speed as might be went about fortification . . .

Captain Newport, having set things in order, set sail for England the 22d of June, leaving provision for thirteen or fourteen weeks. The day before the ship's departure, the king of Pamaunkee sent the Indian that had met us before, in our discovery, to assure us in peace. Our fort being then palisaded round, and all our men in good health and comfort, albeit that through some discontented humors it did not so long continue. God (being angry with us) plagued us with such famine and sickness that the living were scarce able to bury the dead—our want of sufficient good victuals, with continual watching, four or five each night at three bulwarks, being the chief cause. Only of sturgeon had we great store, whereon our men would so greedily surfeit as it cost many lives . . . Shortly after it pleased God, in our extremity, to move the Indians to bring us corn, ere it was half ripe, to refresh us when we rather expected they would destroy us. About the 10th of September there were about forty-six of our men dead . . .

Our provisions being now within twenty days spent, the Indians brought us great store both corn and bread ready-made, and also there came such abundance of fowls into the rivers as greatly refreshed our weak estates, whereupon many of our weak men were presently able to go abroad. As yet we had no houses to cover us, our tents were rotten, and our cabins worse than nought. Our best commodity was iron, which we made into little chisels. The present and Captain Martin's sickness constrained me to be cape merchant, and yet to spare no pains in making houses for the company, who, notwithstanding our misery, little ceased their malice, grudging and muttering.

As at this time most of our chiefest men were either sick or discontented, the rest being in such despair as they would rather starve and rot with idleness than be persuaded to do anything for their own relief without constraint, our victuals being now within eighteen days spent, and the Indian trade decreasing, I was sent to the mouth of the river, to Kegquouhtan and Indian town, to trade for corn and try the river for fish; but our fishing we could not effect by reason of the stormy weather. With fish, oysters, bread, and deer they kindly traded with me and my men.

And now, the winter approaching, the rivers became so filled with swans, geese, ducks, and cranes, that we daily feasted with good bread, Virginia peas, pumpkins, and putchamins fish, fowl, and divers sorts of wild beasts as fat as we could eat them: so that none of tuftaffety humorists desired to go for England.

ECOLOGY Detectives

Built in 1747, the Wells-Thorne House depicts the lifestyle of the residents of Deerfield, Massachusetts, from the early days of 1725 to the 1850s.

We know why a historian would be excited about visiting the Wells-Thorn House, but what would be the attraction for an ecologist? Why would an ecologist—a person who studies the interrelationships of animals, plants, and their surrounding habitats—want to poke around a 275-year-old house? The answer is wood. An ecologist would be able to tell a lot about Deerfield's eighteenth-century environment simply by looking at the wood from which the Wells-Thorn House was built.

History of Trees
The wood tells what types of trees existed in the forests that once surrounded the settlement. For example, the roof shingles are made from rot-resistant cedar, the protective and sturdy clapboards from pine, the interior floor boards and wall paneling from white pine, the strong

One of the oldest trees in Deerfield gets a group hug from at least ten visitors. How many of your friends would it take to encircle the biggest tree in your town?

Historic Deerfield photo

How many things made of wood can you find in this photograph of the parlor in the Wells-Thorn House ell?

ceiling beams from pitch pine or hemlock, and the framework (the house's post and beam) from American chestnut or white oak.

If you have wood walls or floors in your house, measure the width of the boards. Compare your measurement to the width of the wall and floor boards in the Wells-Thorn House, which are twenty-four inches wide. There should be a big difference. Timber beams measure eight inches square. To saw lumber this size, you need to begin with very large trees. If trees were scarce or small in size, the builders would cut smaller beams to make their supply of wood go further, as we do today.

Clues to Colonial Culture

Wood was used for purposes other than house construction. In the kitchen and buttery, hollowed-out logs served as storage bins for grain, butter, and cheese. Baskets were woven from strips of ash. Bowls, plates, and cooking utensils were carved out of wood. Boats, wagons, fence posts and rails, boxes, and barrels also were made of wood.

Of course, the single largest use of wood in colonial times was for the fireplace. This was where all the cooking was done, and it was the only source of heat for the home. To keep fires burning night and day all year long, a family burned about 35 cords of wood (1 cord equals 128 cubic feet). That is approximately 61 tons of wood a year!

Connection from Past to Present

Examples of how wood was used in the Wells-Thorn House and elsewhere show that trees were extremely important to the survival of Deerfield's settlers. They help explain the rapid change in Deerfield's landscape, from forest-covered land to shrubby or open agricultural land. And they help us learn about the connection between landscape and animal habitats. Moose, wolves, fish, and species of birds that once lived in the forests around Deerfield were displaced and driven away as the settlement grew and fields replaced forests.

By combining the knowledge of historical landscape changes with current research, ecologists can create ways to preserve and protect animal populations and habitats. The next time you see an old house or an open field, become an ecological detective and try to imagine what plants and animals may have lived there three hundred years ago. Then think of how the environment might change in another three hundred years.

The single largest use of wood in colonial times was for the fireplace. This was where all the cooking was done, and it was the only source of heat for the home.

© HIP

Historic Deerfield photo

Lazy Settlers

History has not been kind to the first settlers, but there's more to the story.

A "fiasco"—that's what some historians say about the Jamestown settlement effort in 1607. Why? Because, so these people say, the men were lazy and incompetent and the London investors were naive and greedy. These historians also say that the Virginia Company officials did not anticipate the problems the settlers would encounter and that the settlers were incapable of making the venture a success.

Although some of the settlers undoubtedly were poor choices, excavations are providing a more complete view of the early years at Jamestown. The evidence suggests a more positive story than the written accounts reveal.

We also recently learned that the settlers arrived at Jamestown in the midst of a terrible drought. A study of tree rings has shown that it was the driest seven-year period in this region

Sidney King's 1950s painting of Jamestown in 1619.

Identifying the location of the fort and confirming that it was sited strategically on the very best military position on Jamestown Island proves that the settlers had sound military experience. Actually, many of the gentlemen were veterans of the wars the English had fought against the Dutch and had years of experience protecting themselves and fighting in a marshy environment. That the settlers built a timber fort in 19 days in the heat of a Virginia summer was a heroic feat. The design of the trenchwork outside the corners of the fort also reflects expert building skills. That a Confederate fort was built in the same location more than 250 years later also confirms that the first settlers had selected a good site.

There is proof that doctors and surgeons were practicing medicine at Jamestown.

A small piece of human skull (left) found at the site is the earliest known evidence of surgery and autopsy in English America. Cut marks in the bone show that a surgeon attempted to drill holes in the skull to relieve pressure (see illustration bottom). Saw marks on the edge of the bone indicate that an autopsy was performed after the individual died. A variety of medical tools (like some of those shown below) have also been found.

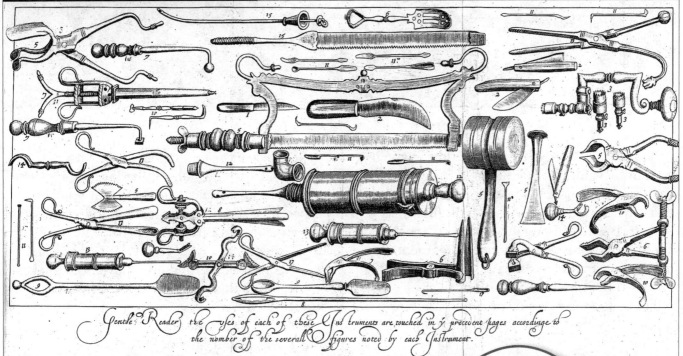

Gentle Reader the uses of each of these Instruments are touched in ye precedent pages according to the number of the severall figures noted by each Instrument.

in nearly 800 years. So, even though the settlers came prepared to trade with the Virginia Indians for food, the supply of available food was limited.

"Starving Time"

The settlement nearly failed after the winter of 1609–1610, the so-called "starving time." The drought was still a problem, and there was not enough food. Less than one third of the people living at the fort survived. The survivors decided to leave and look for food. However, when they met Lord De La Ware with his fleet of supply ships at the mouth of the river, they returned to the fort the next day.

Jamestown went on to become the first permanent English settlement in America and served as the capital of the state of Virginia for almost 100 years.

Fig. 1.

This view of the Jamestown Rediscovery excavations includes the south palisade wall, the south bastion with earth bank "rampart" and nearby "dry moat," with a superimposed digital reconstruction of Fort James.

The original settlers undertook Herculean efforts to build James Fort in only nineteen days.

Preservation Virginia

We are also finding that the settlers adapted some of their English traditions to their new environment. For example, at least three structures appear to have been built first in the English style that used mud and studs (posts). Later renovations used a more environmentally practical post and bark roof construction, the type used by the Indians. Portions of an Indian mat made of reeds, probably used for insulation, were also found in the remains of one building.

It is also clear that the settlers could not match the hunting skills of the Indians and that they had limited meat supplies from England. Apparently, the survivors learned to live mostly on sturgeon and turtle. During the "starving time," they were forced to eat their horses and dogs, as well as rats and even poisonous snakes.

Although the colonists suffered from disease and starvation, they wrapped most of their dead in shrouds, built coffins for some of them, and dug graves to bury them.

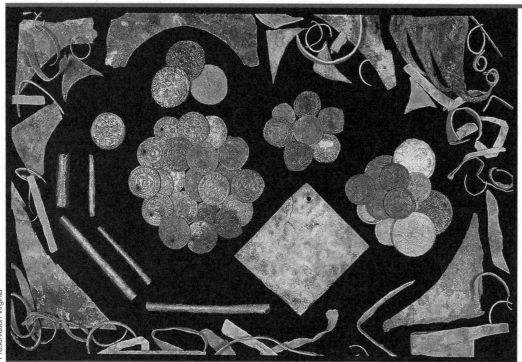

Preservation Virginia

It is clear from the copper, glass beads, and other trade items that the colonists did, at times, try to co-exist peacefully with the Indians.

Before their arrival in Jamestown, the settlers knew the culture of the Indians in the area centered on copper, a material that could be traded for food. Indian pottery with food residue has been found throughout the fort site, and there is evidence that some Indians may have been living in the fort and cooking for the men.

A Jamestown Believer

William Kelso is the director of archaeology for the Association for the Preservation of Virginia Antiquities (APVA) at Historic Jamestowne.

Why did you decide to become an archaeologist?

William Kelso: When I was a high-school history teacher, I started working during the summer and on weekends as an assistant field archaeologist at Colonial Virginia excavation sites. I was taken by the work immediately. I had always fantasized about being able to go back in time and talk to the people who lived in the colonial period. Archaeology was the closest thing I could get to a time machine.

Why is archaeology important?

Kelso: Archaeology makes the story of the past richer and more credible. There's a real honesty in the moment of discovery when you find remains from the past. It's untainted evidence. There aren't the biases that you sometimes see in the written records

and histories. It also tells parts of the story that weren't written about, and gives us a more detailed view of what life was really like in the past.

What is your greatest accomplishment?

Kelso: Finding James Fort and excavating and studying the site with our team of archaeologists is, by far, my greatest accomplishment. Almost everyone thought the site was gone, washed away by the river. More important, Jamestown is so significant to our history. It's really where our nation as we know it today began. I also think the study of the slave quarters at Monticello, the home of Thomas Jefferson, was very important, as it addressed the subject of slavery and the overall structure of the plantation community.

What is your favorite artifact?

Kelso: We found the remains of one of the colonists, and we're pretty sure it's Captain Bartholomew Gosnold. Gosnold was the primary promoter, visionary, and leader of the colony, but he died three months after arriving. Finding his remains may mean that he will finally, after 400 years, receive the recognition he deserves.

Above: William Kelso, left, discusses the James Fort set for *The New World*, a major motion picture about Jamestown that premiered in the fall of 2005, with production designer Jack Fisk.

Right: This engraving shows a contemporary artist's interpretation of Bartholomew Gosnold (right) trading goods with the Indians following his landing in New England in 1602.

A Jamestown Murder Mystery

Preservation Virginia

A grisly find offers an amazing set of clues.

Archaeologists were stunned when they uncovered the grave of a young man (now labeled JR102C, called JR) inside James Fort and found a musket ball embedded in his lower leg. Who was he? Had he shot himself, or did someone shoot him? Was the wound the cause of death?

Ballistics tests with historical weapons have shown that he could not have shot himself. The weapon, which was probably a matchlock, had been fired from too far away. So, someone else must have shot him—accidentally or on purpose. Tests also showed that the musket ball severed an artery and that he bled to death in minutes.

In the early days of the colony, soldiers bearing firearms usually would not wear armor, except for a helmet. However, the above illustration shows JR102C wearing a breastplate, following the new security rules that were passed in 1611.

By Paula Neely, *Dig*, © by Carus Publishing Company. Reproduced with permission.
May be reproduced for classroom use. *Toolkit Texts: Short Nonfiction for American History, Colonial Times*
by Stephanie Harvey and Anne Goudvis, ©2014 (Portsmouth, NH: Heinemann).

Comparisons between radiocarbon dating of a bone sample and other evidence indicate that he died between 1607 and 1620. Because he was buried inside the fort area, it is possible that he was one of the early settlers. It is also likely that he was a gentleman, since he was buried in a coffin. Stains from decayed wood and the positions of coffin nails were the clues to the coffin burial.

Too Much Sugar

By analyzing the skeletal remains, anthropologists learned that he was 5'9", age 17 to 20. Evidence of stress in the joints and ridges where muscles are attached to the bones indicated that he was very active and did strenuous work. His teeth had cavities, suggesting that he probably ate food such as corn or sugar.

The food people eat also leaves clues in their bones that tell where they lived, but the test results for JR are puzzling. If he had lived a long time in Jamestown, tests would indicate that he ate a diet high in corn. If, however, he had lived a long time in England, tests would show that he regularly ate wheat or barley. Surprisingly, JR's test results indicated neither. More important, there is some evidence that before he moved to Jamestown, he may have lived in another region of the world, such as the Caribbean, the Mediterranean, or Africa.

Tooth "Fingerprint"

An analysis of one of his teeth indicates that he may have been born in Wales or the south-western part of England. What a person consumes during infancy leaves a chemical "fingerprint" on the permanent teeth. This "print" can be compared with the same "fingerprint" found in the local groundwater and is used to determine a person's place of birth.

A study of all of the evidence suggests that JR may have been

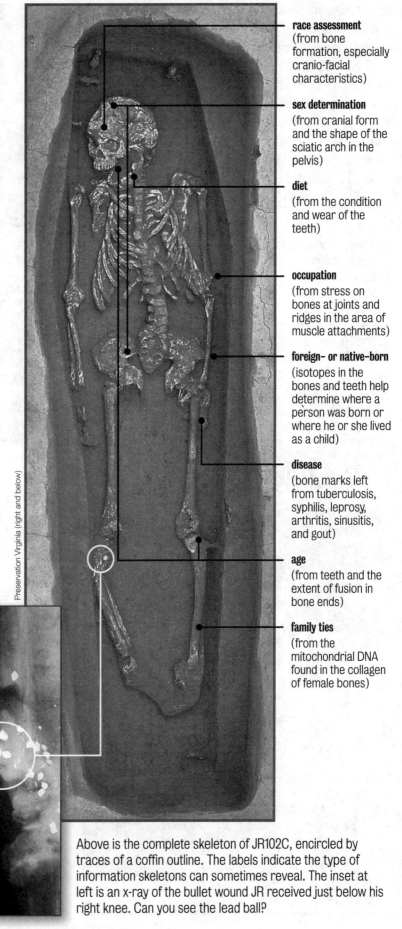

Preservation Virginia (right and below)

race assessment
(from bone formation, especially cranio-facial characteristics)

sex determination
(from cranial form and the shape of the sciatic arch in the pelvis)

diet
(from the condition and wear of the teeth)

occupation
(from stress on bones at joints and ridges in the area of muscle attachments)

foreign- or native-born
(isotopes in the bones and teeth help determine where a person was born or where he or she lived as a child)

disease
(bone marks left from tuberculosis, syphilis, leprosy, arthritis, sinusitis, and gout)

age
(from teeth and the extent of fusion in bone ends)

family ties
(from the mitochondrial DNA found in the collagen of female bones)

Above is the complete skeleton of JR102C, encircled by traces of a coffin outline. The labels indicate the type of information skeletons can sometimes reveal. The inset at left is an x-ray of the bullet wound JR received just below his right knee. Can you see the lead ball?

an English gentleman who moved to Jamestown when he was a young man. He was shot in the leg and died soon after he arrived—sometime between 1607 and 1620. Although there is not yet enough evidence to know for certain who he was, there are several possibilities. One is that he was Jerome Ailcock, a junior officer who, according to the records, died from a "wound" in August 1607. As new tests are developed, archaeologists hope to someday solve the mystery.

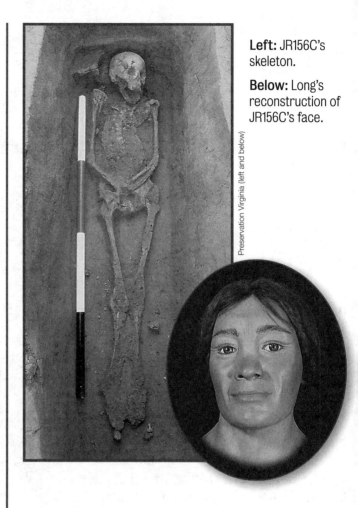

Left: JR156C's skeleton.

Below: Long's reconstruction of JR156C's face.

Below: Anthropologist sculptor Sharon Long checks her measurements and carefully adjusts the sections of her reconstructed face of JR102C.

Right: Long's reconstructed face of JR102C.

"The First Lady"

Found in a grave next to JR, "The First Lady" (officially known as JR156C) died when she was 45 to 55 years old. According to radiocarbon tests, the year was probably sometime between 1620 and 1638. She was 4'8" inches tall and had osteoarthritis of the spinal column, shoulder, and hip. Her bones showed no evidence of doing heavy work during her life.

At the time of her death, she had only five intact teeth, which may mean that she also ate cavity-causing foods such as maize, corn, or sugar over a long period of time. Stains from decayed wood and coffin nails indicate that she was buried in a coffin with a gabled lid. Both the coffin burial and the type of lid suggest that she, like JR, was someone of high social status. The cause of her death is still unknown. Tests on bone samples suggest that she lived in Virginia for an extended period prior to her death, but like JR, it is possible that she may have lived in the Caribbean, the Mediterranean, or Africa before she moved to Jamestown.

Junior Interpreters Enliven Historic Area

*W*arm applause begins as eleven-year-old Annie Goode, costumed as an eighteenth-century girl, plucks the last note of "Greensleeves" on the Geddy House spinet. She performs with the enthusiasm of a child and the poise and polish of a professional. Smoothly, she moves from the brief recital to an engaging presentation on children's games and recreation in Colonial Virginia. It's her second year as a Colonial Williamsburg Foundation junior interpreter, and she enjoys doing what she does well.

"I really like to interact with people and talk about colonial life," Goode says. "I like wearing the costume. And I like playing cricket on the Palace Green."

A student at Williamsburg's Berkeley Middle School, Goode is among 125 students who help, year-round, to bring the eighteenth century to life in the city's restored Historic Area. Colonial Williamsburg is a living history museum that recreates the restored 18th-century capital of Colonial Virginia. They are most evident during the vacation seasons, but they are also on hand for school-year holidays and weekends. Depending on the season, they do historic interpretation at such sites as the Governor's Palace, the Carter's Grove Slave Quarter, the Wythe House, the Brickyard, the Powell House, and the Public Gaol. They demonstrate home gardening, sewing, dancing, housecleaning, singing, and more.

"Visitors like it a lot," says Margaret A. Weiler, director of volunteer programs. "It opens new channels of communication. Children relate to children. When the children are happy, then the parents are happy. The program also is popular with our staff and with our neighbors in the surrounding community."

Children have been part of the Historic Area cast since at least the 1940s, but during the past decade the junior interpreter program has refined their participation to offer more to the youngsters and visitors.

By Ed Crews. May be reproduced for classroom use. *Toolkit Texts: Short Nonfiction for American History, Colonial Times* by Stephanie Harvey and Anne Goudvis, ©2014 (Portsmouth, NH: Heinemann).

Weiler says, "The junior interpreter program allows children to get their first experience in applying for a job, completing a job application, and participating in a job interview. This is an opportunity to experience the road ahead of them as adults. It also is a chance for us to nurture volunteerism, making a commitment to your community and accepting responsibility later in life."

Candidates must be ten to eighteen years old and live near Williamsburg. Prospective junior interpreters complete a questionnaire that tests their communications skills and then are interviewed. Training begins in early spring. New junior interpreters receive about twenty hours of instruction in eighteenth-century Virginia and Williamsburg, including classes on interpretation techniques, children's pastimes and education in the 1700s, chores, household management, period speaking styles, and the proper wearing of costumes. The children also receive instruction related to the historic sites where they will work.

The Colonial Williamsburg staff who coordinate the junior interpreter program say it has a profoundly positive effect on the children who participate. An example is Kerry Vautrot, seventeen. She became a junior interpreter at ten. Since then, she's served as a peer teacher, helping to train young interpreters, and spent last summer working with the Kids' Dig, an educational archaeological program at Carter's Grove. She is now an intern with Colonial Williamsburg's Family Programs and is preparing material for a website.

Vautrot says the junior interpreter program has boosted her self-confidence, helped improve her speaking skills, and given her deep knowledge about colonial life. She says it was fun wearing a costume and developing skill at bilbo, an eighteenth-century game that involves tossing and catching a wooden ball on the end of a stick.

Her experience is helping shape her future. She wants to attend Mary Washington College and major in historic preservation. Vautrot says she's been privileged: "I've had a great opportunity to see a great organization at work."

The Colonial Williamsburg Foundation

I've had a great opportunity to see a great organization at work.

— Kerry Vautrot

By Ed Crews. May be reproduced for classroom use. *Toolkit Texts: Short Nonfiction for American History, Colonial Times* by Stephanie Harvey and Anne Goudvis, ©2014 (Portsmouth, NH: Heinemann).